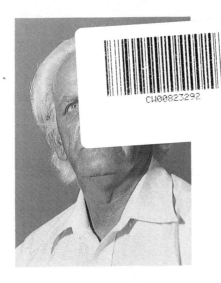

JACK DAVIS was born in Perth in 1917 and brought up at Yarloop and the Moore River native settlements. He first began to learn the language and culture of his people, the Nyoongarah of South-West of Western Australia, while living on the Brookton Aboriginal Reserve. He later worked as a stockman in the North-West which brought him into contact with tribal society.

He became an activist on behalf of his people and from 1967-71 was director of the Aboriginal Centre in Perth. In 1971 he became the first chairman of the Aboriginal Trust in West Australia and from 1972-77 was managing editor of the Aboriginal Publications Foundation. He was a member of the Institute of Aboriginal Studies in Canberra and established a course for Aboriginal writers at Murdoch University. He was also a member of the Aboriginal Arts Board of the Australia Council.

His first full-length play, *Kullark*, a documentary on the history of Aboriginals in West Australia, was first presented in 1979. It was followed by *The Dreamers* (1983), which toured Australia under the auspices of the Australian Elizabethan Theatre Trust. Following the success of this tour, the Trust commissioned *No Sugar* for the 1985 Festival of Perth and *Honey Spot*, a children's play, for the 1985 Come Out Festival in Adelaide. In 1986 *No Sugar* was re-mounted by the Trust for a season at the World Theatre Festival in Vancouver.

For services to his people Jack Davis received the British Empire Medal in 1977; in 1985 he became a member of the Order of Australia, received the Sydney Myer Performing Arts Award, an Hon. D.Litt from Murdoch University and was elected Citizen of the Year in West Australia. In 1986 *No Sugar* was co-winner of the Australian Writers Guild award for the best stage play of the year.

Jack Davis died in March 2000.

The Dreamers

Jack Davis

Currency Press • Sydney

CURRENCY PLAYS

First published in 1982 with *Kullark* by
Currency Press Pty Ltd,
PO Box 2287, Strawberry Hills NSW 2012 Australia
enquiries@currency.com.au; www.currency.com.au

Revised edition 1984, Reprinted 1984, 1988

This single edition first published in 1996

Reprinted 1998, 1999, 2001, 2002

Copyright © Jack Davis 1982

Copying for Educational Purposes

The Australian *Copyright Act* 1968 (Act) allows a maximum of one chapter or 10% of this book, whichever is the greater, to be copied by an educational institution for its educational purposes provided that that educational institution (or the body that administers it) has given a remuneration notice to Copyright Agency Limited (CAL) under the Act. For details of the CAL licence for educational institutions contact CAL, 19/157 Liverpool Street, Sydney NSW 2000. Tel: (02) 9394 7600; Fax: (02) 9394 7601; E-mail: info@copyright.com.au.

Copying for Other Purposes:

Except as permitted under the Act, for example a fair dealing for the purposes of study, research, criticism or review, no part of this book may be reproduced, stored in a retrieval system, or transmitted in any form or by any means without prior written permission. All enquiries should be made to the publisher at the above address.

Any performance or public reading of *The Dreamers* is forbidden unless a licence has been received from the author's agent. The purchase of this book in no way gives the purchaser the right to perform the play in public, whether by means of a staged production or a reading. All applications for public performance should be addressed to Currency Press.

National Library of Australia Cataloguing-in-Publication data:
Davis, Jack, 1917–
   The dreamers
   ISBN 0 86819 454 9
   I. Title.
A822.3

Cover photograph shows Lynette Narkle and Jack Davis, as Dolly and Uncle Worru, in the National Theatre Company production on tour, 1983. (Photo: Geoffrey Lovell)

Printed by Southwood Press, Marrickville.

Contents

The Dreamers was first performed by the Swan River Stage Company at the Dolphin Theatre, Perth, on 2 February 1982 with the following cast:

WORRU	Jack Davis
DOLLY	Lynette Narkle
MEENA	Maxine Narkle
SHANE	John Pell
ROY	Michael Fuller
ELI	Trevor Parfitt
PETER	Luke Fuller
DARREN	Shane McIntyre
ROBERT	Wayne Bynder
DANCER	Michael T. Fuller

Didgeridoo music played by Richard Walley
Lighting and set design by Keith Edmundson
Choreography by Richard Walley
Directed by Andrew Ross

CHARACTERS

UNCLE WORRU, an old Aboriginal
DOLLY, his niece
MEENA, her daughter, aged fourteen
SHANE, her son, aged twelve
ROY, her husband
ELI, a cousin
PETER, her son, aged eighteen
DARREN, a white boy, about twelve years old
ROBERT, Dolly's nephew
DANCER, a tribal dancer

SETTING

The action takes place over six months in the home of the Wallitch family, in South-Western Australia. The time is the present.

ACT ONE

BEERUK – SUMMER

SCENE ONE

Dawn. We hear the distant echoing voices of children singing a tribal song.

A tribal family walks slowly across the escarpment silhouetted against the first light of dawn. The men lead, carrying weapons, the women and children follow with bags, kulumans and fire sticks. As they disappear the voices fade and a narrow beam of light reveals WORRU *alone downstage.*

WORRU   I walked down the track
to where the camp place used to be
and voices, laughing, singing
came surging back to me.

It was situated on the Swan
not far from the old homestead.
That's gone too.
Kindly old man Hammersley,
they can stay there as long as they like,
he said.
Now he too is dead.
Billy Kimberley used to corroboree
there weekends
for a tin of Lucky Hit,
then share it with his friends.

Now we who were there
who were young,
are now old and live in suburbia,
and my longing is an echo

a re-occurring dream,
coming back along the track
from where the campfires used to gleam

Then there was Angie,
twenty-two stone.
Proud she and Herbie was proper given
church married not-livin'.
Meal times,
Bella pulling the damper like a golden moon
from the ashes of the fire,
then sharing the last of the bacca,
some with clay pipes
and others rolling.

Now we who were there
who were young,
are now old and live in suburbia,
and my longing is an echo
a re-occurring dream,
coming back along the track
from where the campfires used to gleam.

The spotlight on WORRU *fades*

SCENE TWO

Early morning – a hot, still summer morning. The sound of warbling magpies and children.

In the living room ROY *sits lethargically reading the paper.* COUSIN ELI *is pencilling selections on the racing page while* DOLLY *prepares bread, butter and tea for breakfast. A large battered saucepan of water begins to boil on the stove. Eventually* DOLLY *peers into it and calls out in a piercing voice.*

DOLLY   Come on, you kids. Hurry up, water's ready.

MEENA   I'm having it first.

MEENA *and* SHANE *enter arguing*

SHANE   No you're not, I am.

MEENA   I am! You can have it after.

SHANE   [*pushing past* MEENA] You didn't wash before breakfast, you might as well go to school without one.

MEENA   Listen who's talkin', when you wash you don't even get wet anyhow.

SHANE   I do so.

MEENA   You might as well use spit.

>   MEENA *grabs the saucepan off the stove and* SHANE *pushes her. Water splashes onto the floor.*

>   [*running off with the saucepan.*] Watch it, Shane.

SHANE   [*chasing her*] You're spilling it all.

>   MEENA *and* SHANE *exit.*

DOLLY   You two be careful.

MEENA   [*off*] Was Shane's fault.

DOLLY   Shut yer trap both of yer –

SHANE   [*off*] 'S her fault' –

DOLLY   – and share the water.

>   DOLLY *places a mug of tea and some buttered bread in front of* ROY. *The commotion continues offstage.*

SHANE   Save some for me.

MEENA   All right.

SHANE   Don't use it all, like you always do.

MEENA   I'm not, get out of the road.

SHANE   Mum said you gotta share it.

MEENA   Yeah, well give us the soap.

SHANE   All right, here ya are. Give us some water.

MEENA   Careful Shane.

SHANE   Watch it!

>   *The sound of screaming, the saucepan crashing to the floor.* DOLLY *rushes out after them,* ROY *looks up from his paper.*

DOLLY   Oh gawd! What happened?

MEENA   I had it first.

SHANE   She wouldn't leave me any.

DOLLY   You're lucky you never burnt yourselves.

SHANE   It wasn't my fault.

DOLLY   [*returning*] All right you can wash in cold water now and you can mop up the mess. [*To* ROY.] Oh gawd, I wish we 'ad a decent place to live in. No hot water, no locks on the doors, worse than livin' in a bloody camp.

ROY *retreats into the newspaper.*

Why don't you go down the Road Board? They'd put you on. Cousin William got a job there.

MEENA *enters, saunters across the room and collects a balding mop. She exits.*

They've even got a *Nyoongah* bloke drivin' the garbage truck.

ELI   Yeah, an' they do all right sellin' bottles an' things, 'sides their wages.

ROY   Well, why don't you go down an' see 'em for a job, then ?

ELI   For me or for you Unc?

DOLLY   [*to* ROY] You? If you weren't so bloody bone tired we'd get a good 'ouse an' good furniture.

MEENA   [*off*] Give it to me!

SHANE   [*off*] No!

MEENA   [*off*] I had it first.

MEENA *appears at the door.*

Mum, Shane won't give me the comb. Mum, make him give it to me.

DOLLY   Shane, give it to her and shut up, the both of you.

SHANE *enters pushing roughly past* MEENA.

SHANE   All right, then I won't comb my hair.

He hurls the comb at MEENA.

You can keep your stinkin' old comb.

DOLLY   Oh, what difference does it make? You can still use it after.

SHANE   What, after her? Don't want none of her nits.

ELI   [*producing a comb*] 'Ere, use mine.

       SHANE *painfully combs the knots out of his hair.*

       You oughta get it cut, you're startin' to look like a *yorga*.

SHANE   Shut yer mouth, cousin Eli, you're only jealous 'cause you look like a fuzzy mop walking down the street. Wonder the cops don't turn you upside and use you for a mop down the lock up on a Sunday morning.

DOLLY   That'll do, that's enough.

       SHANE *throws the comb to* ELI, *grabs several slices of bread and slouches off.*

       You shut up, Eli, an' think about washin' yourself. I want you to come down the 'ospital with me to pick up Uncle Worru.

ELI   Aw, come on Auntie, I had trouble with me eye all night.-

ROY   Urgh! Eye, me *kwon.*

DOLLY   Ah, don't worry about it. I'll go on me own. [*Pointing to* ROY.] I can see you're related to 'im.

MEENA   [*entering neat and tidy, school bag in hand*] Mum, that isn't a *Nyoongah* driving the garbage truck, 'es an Indian bloke.

DOLLY   What of it, still coloured, ain't he?

ROY   Lot of difference, he ain't a *Nyoongah* an' that's good enough for me.

       PETER *enters, ambling across the front of the stage.*

MEENA   [*imperiously*] As a matter of fact there's very little difference. They are very much like Aborigines because that's where we come from, India. We came across the land bridge, then the sea came behind us and Australia was iso... isolated and the only animal we brought with us was the dingo.

DOLLY   All right, Miss *Wetjala*, git goin' to school.

       MEENA *leaves, pulling* ELI*'s hair.*

MEENA   Bye, fuzzy top, bye.

          MEENA *leaves, but returns to the doorway.*

          Peter's comin'.

          MEENA *exits.*

DOLLY   [*pointing at* ROY] You wanna check that boy.

ROY   Aw, 'es old enough to look after 'imself.

          PETER *appears in the doorway.*

          Where d'you git to last night?

PETER   Aw, I stopped out at Auntie Peggy's.

ELI   [*grinning*] *Bunjin'* around, I bet.

PETER   You're only jealous, anyway.

DOLLY   You sure you was at Auntie Peggy's?

PETER   Yeah, course I was.

DOLLY   Well 'ow d'ya git 'ere?

PETER   She gave me a bus fare.

DOLLY   Next time you stay out, you let me know.

PETER   OK.

ELI   [*miming handcuffs*] I thought you was *woonana*.

          DOLLY *pours him a cup of tea.*

PETER   Was you afraid I mighta 'ad your favourite cell?

ELI   [*laughing*] Which one's that?

ROY   He's got his name scratched in all of 'em.

ELI   Yeah, Sergeant thought about puttin' a brass name plate on
          the door for me; Elijah William Zakariah Wallitch.

ROY   Jacky, you mean.

ELI   Yeah, Elijah William Zakariah Wallitch, Jacky.

          They laugh.

DOLLY   And how's Auntie Peggy?

PETER   Aw, she's all right.

DOLLY   The boy's 'ome?

PETER   Yeah, Big mob there, Northam lot came down Friday, they was still there when I left.

ROY   Hope they don't come round lookin' for *boondah* for petrol to git 'ome.

ELI   [*smacking his pockets*] Won't be gettin' any *boondah* out of me. [*Gesturing nothing.*] 'Cause I'm like that.

PETER   Don't you know how to milk a bowser?

ELI   [*shrugging his shoulders*] Nah.

ROY   [*feigning surprise*] Oh Eli, now, that's hard to believe.

PETER   It's easy, all you gotta do is pick the lock, then you gotta switch –

DOLLY   [*interrupting, flicking him*] That'll do from you. If you wanta pick anythin' you can come down with me an' pick up Uncle Worru.

PETER   Aw, Mum, I'm feeling a bit tired. Those fellas kept me awake all night talkin' an' playin' cards. Gawd, they're a rowdy lot.

DOLLY   If you'd come home, you'd a gotta decent sleep.

        DOLLY *slams a handful of money on the table and addresses* ROY.

        An' you can go down the butcher an' git some flaps an' bread an' 'ave it cooked for the kids at lunchtime. I'm goin' to pick up Uncle Worru and send him home in a taxi. An' you two clean up, an' clean up properly.

        ROY *produces cigarette butts and breaks them open for tobacco.*

ROY   'Ow about some *gnummari*?

DOLLY   Get yourself a job and you'll have plenty a smokes.

ROY   Aw, come on love. Gimme another forty cents an' I'll 'ave enough for a packet.

DOLLY   You got enough here for papers; it won't hurt you to pick up a few butts, an' it won't be the first time.

ROY   An' it won't be the bloody last.

        They sit in silence. DOLLY *walks purposefully across the stage and exits.* ROY *finds a longish butt, attempts to light up and lets out a deep hacking chest cough.*

ELI   Well, what's on the programme for today?

Silence.

Anybody got any ideas?

Silence.

How about a bottle of *gnoop*?

ROY   Bloody good idea. Take this cough off me chest.

ELI   [*looking at the money*] If we 'ad some *boondah*?

ROY   No *choo*. Can't use this, gotta git tucker.

ELI   Plenty time to scrounge for tucker, it's early yet, sun just up in the air. Don't worry, ol' Hawkeye'll 'ave some money by lunchtime.

They look at each other guiltily until ROY *finally throws the money in the centre of the table.*

ROY   All right, who's goin' to go?

PETER   Well, I'm not goin' to the Exchange, anyway.

ELI   Why not?

PETER   Fuckin' barman put me outa there last night.

ROY   What? You got as much right as anybody else.

ELI   What for?

PETER   Aw, he reckon I king hit that *Wetjala* bloke in the *goonamia* Friday night.

ELI   What bloke?

PETER   You know that big ding bloke with the bendy back?

ELI   That bloke. He's always hangin' around *Nyoongah*, he's only a gin tailer. Fancy refusin' a man a drink over scum like him; bastard deserved all he got.

PETER   Yeah, an' I give it to him, flattened him, [*miming a heavy punch*] *bukily*. Put 'im right down in the *koomp*.

ROY   [*miming handcuffs*] You wanna watch it.

PETER   All right, gimme the money.

PETER *collects the money and swaggers towards the*

door.

ROY   You better keep away from the Exchange.

PETER   Yeah, I'll go to the grog shop.

ELI   [*calling*] Git port.

          PETER *walks across the stage counting the money.*

ROY   And don't forget cigarette papers.

ELI   And some butts.

          The lights fade as PETER *exits.*

SCENE THREE

A distant ambulance siren, the hollow footsteps and clatter of a hospital corridor.

A pool of light reveals WORRU, *dressed in a second-hand suit, but without shoes, sitting awkwardly on a hospital bed. An old suitcase stands at the end of the bed. Eventually* DOLLY *enters.*

DOLLY   'Ullo Uncle Worru. [*Kissing him.*] I come to get you. You ready to come 'ome?

WORRU   Yeah, where you bin? I bin waitin' all mornin' for you.

DOLLY   Sorry Uncle, I got here quick as I could. Eh, where d'ya get your new clothes from?

WORRU   Sister give 'em to me; she get 'em from Red Cross.

          He shows off a new white handkerchief.

DOLLY   And new 'anky.

WORRU   New sockses too; pretty ones.

DOLLY   Where's your shoes?

          WORRU *points under the bed.*

WORRU   There somewheres.

          He bends down and almost topples off the bed.

DOLLY   Woops, careful, careful, you gonna look like a real *bridaira*. Lift your foot up. [*Putting on his shoes.*] They won't know you when you get home.

WORRU   Who's 'ome?

DOLLY   Oh, just our lot, they all sittin' around like that.

> DOLLY *indicates they are broke, by making a circle with her thumb and index finger.*

WORRU   What, Eli got *boondah*?

DOLLY   No, he's *koorawoorliny*.

WORRU   *Koorawoorliny*, what's wrong with ol' Hawkeye?

DOLLY   He's got 'em, 'e goes for the big kill Thursdays, late night shopping. Stand up now, Unc, see if your shoes are all right.

> WORRU *stands up and flicks imaginary dust off his clothes with his handkerchief.* DOLLY *straightens his clothes.*

Right, where's your bag?

> *He points, she picks it up and looks inside.*

You got your old clothes in here. What's this?

> *She holds up a slice of toast.*

WORRU   Toast. I save from breakfast.

DOLLY   [*laughing*] What for?

WORRU   I allus git *kobble weert* 'fore lunchtime.

DOLLY   Uncle Worru! Now you feel all right to walk home?

WORRU   *Kia*, I feel good.

DOLLY   No-o-oh. I think I betta get a taxi for you. I gotta go and pay the rent.

WORRU   [*stamping his feet*] No, I wanna *tjen kooliny*, stretch my *marta*. I'm *moorditj*.

DOLLY   No, taxi for you, old fella. You gotta stay *moorditj*. No more drink for you, or you be right back 'ere in this bed again.

WORRU   No, not comin' back 'ere. Next time I go to *Nyoongah* doctor, *boolyaduk*, Pinjarra. Get too many needles in this place. They no good, *warrah*.

DOLLY   Well, you ready? We gotta go an' see sister now before you leave.

WORRU   You go, I wait out 'ere.

DOLLY   No, Unc. Sister wants to talk to you, tell you about your medicine, and comin' back for a check up.

WORRU   No, not comin' back 'ere.

DOLLY   [*laughing*] Why don't you want to see her? She's been real nice to you.

>   WORRU *shakes his head.*

>   Why don't you wanna see her?

WORRU   She might wanna give me 'nother needle.

DOLLY   [*laughing*] Oh, come on, Unc, you're finish with them now.

WORRU   I go this way.

>   *He moves away, but* DOLLY *steers him back the other way.*

DOLLY   Come on, Unc, steady, steady, walk *dubbakiny* now.

>   DOLLY *gently shepherds* WORRU *off.*

WORRU   Needles, needles. [*Pointing to his arm.*] In 'ere, in 'ere [*pointing to his side*] an' in there; [*pointing to his posterior*] an' in there. I feel like a bloody *nyngarn*.

>   *They exit.*

SCENE FOUR

The hospital sounds give way to a noisy argument as light builds on the kitchen area.

   PETER, ROY, WORRU *and* ELI *sit around the table drinking. Two bottles stand on the table, one empty, the other full.*

ELI   [*shouting*] Freeo? What's wrong with Fremantle Gaol?

PETER   What's wrong with it?

ELI   You git three meals a day and a hot shower. Not like this place.

ROY   Ay, an' how you gunna git on for a drink?

ELI   Yuh can git a boot polish cocktail now and again.

ROY   You and your boot polish cocktail, bloody paint thinners. That's what killing those stupid black bastards down there, not what they're gittin' 'round the back.

ELI   Bullshit! I still reckon they knocked old Sandy off and dumped him back in the cell. Look you blokes, I'm tellin' yuh, Sandy was as tough as an old boomer. Slept under bridges, ate 'ard tucker all 'is life. Heart failure, be buggered; number nines killed 'im, that's for sure.

PETER OK, number nines knocked him off. But how you gonna prove it?

ELI   You can't prove nothin', 'cause them screws are too bloody smart for dumb blackfellas.

PETER It's not because they're too smart, there's just too bloody many of them.

ROY   Ah, bullshit!

PETER Look, *Nyoongahs* buy their grog from *Wetjalas*, they break the law and they git jugged by *Wetjalas*. The lawyer's white, the cops are white, the magistrate's white, the warden's white, the whole box and dice is white. Put a *Nyoongah* against all them. I tell you we ain't got a bloody chance.

ELI   Warders, they're no trouble. I know 'ow to handle them bastards: 'yes sir, no, Warden. I'll do it, sir.' All you gotta do is butter 'em up a bit. Play it smart.

PETER Playin' along with the system eh?

ROY   Arse lickin' I call it, you're just scareda gettin' belted up.

       ELI *stands up and thumps the table.*

ELI   Look at this – busted eye, broken nose, busted eardrum, [*pointing to his head*] thirteen stitches! You know who done all that? Not *Wetjalas*, but *Nyoongahs*, me own fuckin' people!

PETER   Man, yer wrong, the system done that to yuh, but yuh can't see it.

ROY   How d'yuh expect him to see it, 'es only got one eye, so 'e reckons.

         They laugh. WORRU *pushes his chipped enamel mug across to* PETER.

WORRU   Come on, boy, gimme *kaep*, gimme *kaep*.

PETER   [*taking the bottle away*] No, Pop, I think you had enough. You know you just come outa hospital.

ELI   Aw, come on. Give the poor ol' fella a drink. One drink won't 'urt 'im. [*Pouring him a drink.*] 'Ere y' are, oldy, git that inta yuh.

PETER   Gee, Pop, you look real smart in them new clothes.

         He picks WORRU*'s jacket off the floor. His pills fall unnoticed onto the floor.*

WORRU   Nurse gib 'em to me. She pretty one too.

         He cackles cheekily.

ELI   Yeah. Bet you could tell some stories 'bout you an' them nurses, eh?

WORRU   Yeah! I tell 'em a lotta stories. I tell 'em that one 'bout Cornell an' Milbart, on the train. An' they laugh somethin' cruel. [*Laughing.*] Roy! You know that one.

ROY   No, never heard that one, Pop.

WORRU   Yeah, you know.

ELI   No 'e don't, Unc. Come on, what 'appened?

ROY   Yeah, Unc, tell us the yarn.

WORRU   Well, they was gitten old fellas, them two, Cornell and Milbart, they was stayin' in Wagin an' they wanted to git to Katanning Show, see? And they was *wayarning* of the train, real *wayarning*. [*Laughing.*] Anyways, they got in a railway carriage and that train was goin' *keert kooliny, keert kooliny* round them bends and them corners. An' – an' – they was... they was...

         He coughs and splutters.

... sitting close together, like.

He laughs again and claps his hands.

Anyway, they went around one corner and Cornell got a real fright and he shouted '*choo*' and he pushed Milbart like that.

He pushes PETER *almost off his seat.*

And he said, he said, '*Wart arny yit*, Milbart, git ober in de udder corner an' help me balance this thing before it bloody tips over.'

They all laugh, WORRU *coughs.*

Ay, boy, give me 'nother drink. 'Urry up, come on!

PETER   Aw right, Pop, but you gotta tell us another yarn now.

WORRU   Aw right, yeah.

He stops suddenly.

ELI   Yeah, come on, Pop.

WORRU   By rights I shouldn' be tellin' you fellas this. [*Pointing to* ROY.] Aw right for 'im.

ROY   It's all right Unc.

WORRU   All right. Well, you know that Christmas tree, that's the *moodgah*, that's the *Nyoongah* name.

PETER   Yeah?

WORRU   Well, when our people was *noych*, their *kunya* – that's what *Wetjala* call soul, *unna*?

ROY   Yeah, that's right, Uncle.

WORRU   Well their *kunya* would go and stay in the *moodgah* tree, some time for a l-o-o-ng time, an' when the *moodgah* flowers were gone, summertime, their *kunya* would leave the *moodgah* an' go to Watjerup. That way, over the sea, Watjerup, thaty way, *boh-oh*.

He gestures westward. His audience is mesmerised.

PETER   Where's Watjerup, Popeye?

WORRU   *Kia*, Watjerup, that's what *Wetjulas* call Rottnest. An' if you go Mogumber old settlement, lotta *moodgah* up there

'cause, 'cause that be *Nyoongah* country for lo-o-ng time.
An' them *moodgah* they strong, they kill other tree if they
grow near them, *bantji, muttlegahruk, tjarraly, kudden*, kill
'em, finish, 'cause *kunyas* make him strong an' only
boolya man can go there near the *moodgah* 'cause the
boolya man is strong too, like that tree; an' 'e can drink
water an' take 'oney from the *moodgah*. Anybody else,
that's *warrah*, they could be finish, *unna*?

> *An eerie silence overcomes them.* PETER *shudders and
> jumps up.*

PETER Come on, this is gettin' too morbid. Let's have some
bloody music.

> *They relax and pour drinks.* PETER *turns the radio on
> and begins to dance drunkenly.*

WORRU [*laughing*] Ah, you don't call that dancin', do you?

ELI Go on, Pop, git up an' show 'im a real *middar*. Go on,
oldy, a real dinkum *yahllarah*.

WORRU Awright, awright, I'll show you fellas, me an' Nindal we
danced for the Prince of New South Wales.

> WORRU *rises and begins a drunken stumbling version of
> a half-remembered tribal dance.* PETER *turns the
> volume up and continues his own disco dance.* WORRU
> *pushes him aside and dances to the amusement of* ELI
> *and* ROY, *until his feet tangle and he falls heavily.*
>
> *The scene freezes, the light changes, and the radio cuts
> abruptly to heavy rhythmic didgeridoo and clap sticks.
> An intricately painted* DANCER *appears on the
> escarpment against a dramatic red sky, dances down
> and across in front of them, pounding his feet into the
> stage. Finally, he dances back up the ramp where he
> poses for a moment before the light snaps out on the
> last note of music.*

SCENE FIVE

About an hour later. The full bottle is now nearly empty. The heat and the alcohol are taking their toll. WORRU, *now dishevelled, is slumped on the sofa asleep. His handkerchief, shoes and socks lie about the room.* ROY *and* ELI *are half asleep around the table,* PETER *is leaning over the sink gazing blankly through the window. The occasional crow can be heard.*

The stillness is eventually broken by PETER *splashing himself with water.* SHANE *enters, wearily drags his feet across the stage, goes inside and opens the fridge.* MEENA *follows.*

SHANE   Gawd I'm hungry, what's for lunch? [*Spotting* WORRU.] Oh hi, Pop, how are you?

MEENA   Hello Pop, you look super. New clothes? You look real *moorditj.*

WORRU   *Kia gnullarah bridaira nyinning.*

         They laugh.

SHANE   Oh crikey, what's for lunch?

MEENA   You should have got them to shave your beard off.

WORRU   *Yuart! Yuart!*

SHANE   Anything to eat?

MEENA   Where's Mum?

PETER   She's in town, shopping. She'll be back directly.

SHANE   What's the good of that, we'll be back at school by then.

MEENA   And still hungry.

ROY   [*pointing*] Bread there, butter there, some cool drink in the fridge.

         SHANE *gets a near empty bottle of Coca-Cola from the fridge.* MEENA *tips a stale crust from the bread packet, she butters it, glaring at the wine bottles.*

MEENA   Why didn't Mum leave us some lunch money?

ELI   [*guiltily*] She's gone to town to get bread and meat.

SHANE   [*emptying his pockets*] I got – ah – nine cents. Anyone build on that? Enough to get a pie.

           He *tries* ROY, then ELI.

ELI   Aw, we're open.

MEENA   [*picking up the nearly-empty wine bottle*] Looks like it.

           ELI *points to* WORRU *who has dozed off.* SHANE *shuffles across to him and wakes him gently.*

SHANE   Hey, Popeye, Popeye.

WORRU   [*waking*] Ay, ay, what d'ya want?

SHANE   You got any money to put with this, enough for a pie, Popeye?

WORRU   Ay, what's the matter, boy?

SHANE   I want to get a pie for lunch, I'm hungry.

WORRU   Yeah, here you are.

           Coins fall to the floor. SHANE *swoops on them.*

SHANE   Oh boy – nine, ten, thirty, forty, fifty, fifty cents. Wow, got enough! Saved from starvation.

MEENA   Sure you got enough?

SHANE   Yeah, enough for one, anyway.

MEENA   Thank you, Popeye Worru, see you later.

SHANE   Thanks Pop, see you!

           They sprint out. MEENA *stops* SHANE *as he runs across the stage, grabbing him by the shirt.*

MEENA   Half each, remember.

SHANE   Yeah, I know. Come on.

           They run off. The men sit in silence. PETER *wanders across to the table and drops into a chair.* ELI *holds up the nearly-empty bottle and peers into it.* WORRU *dozes off again.*

ELI   Not much left. Nearly finished.

ROY   Well, if we got none, we go without.

ELI *edges across to the sofa and wakes* WORRU.

ELI   Hey Pop, *boondah wah*?

WORRU   Ay, what?

ELI   You got any *boondah*?

      WORRU *pretends to sleep.*

PETER   *Choo kynya*, you got no shame, Eli. Poor old fella.

ELI   Nah, it's all right. I'll give it back to him Thursday night. Pop, you got some *boondah* and I'll go and get another bottle of port for us.

      WORRU *starts to go through his pockets.*

      Look in this one.

      He goes to search WORRU *but* WORRU *pushes him away.*

WORRU   What do you think I can't see? I got two eyes not like you, *meowl birt.*

      ELI *laughs.*

ELI   Oops, sorry Pop.

ROY   Don't worry about him, Uncle, he's got two eyes.

      WORRU *gives* ELI *a handful of change.*

WORRU   'Ere. And don't forget bring me some *gnummari*. You 'ear me?

ELI   Sure, Pop, sure. Now let's see how much we got. [*Counting.*] Bastard.

PETER   What?

ELI   Fifty cents short.

PETER   Hang on, hang on.

      He goes through his pockets and drops a fifty-cent piece on the table.

ELI   Where did you get that from?

PETER   Auntie Peggy gave it to me for a bus fare.

ROY   I thought you said you came home on the bus this morning.

PETER   I did! But when the driver asked for my fare I made out I lost it. He was going to put me off at the next stop but this old *Wetjula* lady paid my fare.

> ELI *slips the nearly-empty bottle into his pocket, unnoticed by* ROY *or* WORRU, *pulls his eyepatch over his eye and does a curious comical shuffle towards the door.*

ELI   Right, move your black feet, Eli Wallitch, move your black feet. [*To* PETER.] You comin?

PETER   Yeah, might as well.

ROY   Don't be long. Get back here before the old girl gits home.

> ELI *and* PETER *step briskly across the stage.* ELI *shows* PETER *the bottle. They exit quickly laughing.* ROY *empties his glass and looks about for the bottle, first bewildered then frantic. He rushes to the door.*

Eli! Eli! [*Walking back inside.*] You fuckin' sly dingo bastard!

WORRU   Who? Who you *warrah wangeing*?

ROY   Oh that bloody Eli.

WORRU   *Nietjuk*?

ROY   He beats me every fuckin' time.

> WORRU *dozes off.* ROY *makes a half-hearted attempt to clean up the kitchen, carefully concealing the empty bottle behind the fridge.*

Hey Pop, Pop.

WORRU   What, what?

ROY   You go lay down for a while.

WORRU   Ay ?

ROY   Why don't you have a bit of a rest?

WORRU   *Kia, kia*, I think I will.

> ROY *helps him to his feet and steers him towards the door.* WORRU *staggers out and flops onto his bed.*

ROY   Old girl will be home directly and she'll cook us a feed.

> ROY *sits at the table, puts his feet up and closes his*

eyes. WORRU *begins to grunt and mumble incoherently, gradually becoming clearer and building to a shout.*

WORRU   *Kia* Milbart, Milbart! Where is water, *kaep wah*?

SCENE SIX

Mid afternoon. It is oppressively hot and still. WORRU *is fast asleep sprawled on his bed.* ROY, *also asleep, lolls precariously on a chair with his feet on the table. The slow rhythmic breathing of the sleepers is punctuated by the occasional crow.*

DOLLY, *carrying a bulging supermarket bag, trudges wearily across the stage. As she enters the house she stops and surveys the room before creeping in and putting down the groceries. She picks up a mug, sniffs it, rinses it and uses it to drink water. She peers inquisitively about the room, then behind the fridge, where she discovers the wine bottle. Finally, she steals alongside* ROY, *gently nudges him off his chair and sits down as he drops limply onto the floor. Roy wakes in terror, jumps up and looks around the room.*

ROY   Awgh! What the fuck! Oooh! [*Spotting* DOLLY.] Aw, 'ullo love.

          Pause.

          'Ow you going?

DOLLY   [*coolly*] I'm all right.

          Pause.

          Where's the boys?

          She begins to unpack the groceries.

ROY   What?

DOLLY   Peter an' Eli.

ROY   Oh, they down town somewheres.

DOLLY   Kids been 'ome?

ROY   Yeah, they bin 'ome.

DOLLY   They 'ave lunch, eh?

ROY   Yeah, yeah, yeah.

DOLLY   What they 'ave?

ROY   They 'ad pies an' cool drink.

DOLLY   Didn't you get to the butcher's shop?

ROY   No, they 'ad pies instead.

DOLLY   How's ole fella?

ROY   Oh 'es sleepin, 'es been asleep all mornin'.

           She looks about and picks up UNCLE WORRU*'s pills,
           handkerchief, shoes and socks.*

DOLLY   How did these get 'ere?

ROY   Aw, I dunno!

DOLLY   And how'd this get 'ere?

           She picks up the empty bottle.

           Now where did you git the money from?

ROY   What money?

DOLLY   For this bloody bottle?

ROY   Oh, Eli bought it this morning.

           He starts to feel around for his thongs.

DOLLY   [*threatening him with the bottle*] Roy Wallitch, you're a
           rotten stinkin' liar. You spent the kids' dinner money on
           this, didn't you?

ROY   I tell you Eli an' Peter got it.

           He starts to get up.

DOLLY   You're not only useless, you're a bloody liar as well. You
           spent the kids' dinner money, didn't you? Didn't you?

ROY   Shit, I'm gettin' outa 'ere.

DOLLY   You bastard!

           ROY *bolts for the door,* DOLLY *makes to throw the bottle
           at him but thinks better of it. She walks across to the
           table and drops wearily into a chair.* ROY *hops across
           the stage with one thong, stops with a yell, rubs his foot
           painfully.*

ROY   Bloody doublegees!

             He puts his thong on and gallops off. WORRU, *awoken
             by the commotion, rises and stumbles half asleep and
             half drunk into the doorway.*

WORRU   Ay? Ay? Ay? What's goin' on.

DOLLY   Ts, ts, ts! Just look at you, 'ome from the hospital two
             hours and you're drunk already. 'Ave you taken your pills?

             *He clumsily feels in his pockets, then shrugs his
             shoulders.*

WORRU   Must be there somewheres.

             *She picks them up off the table and gets a glass of
             water. He walks across and sits down, doing his best to
             appear sober.*

DOLLY   I dunno what I'm gonna do with you, looks like you wanna
             die, eh?

WORRU   Aw, leave me alone.

DOLLY   You'll be all alone down in the cemetery.

WORRU   I don't care, you can chuck me on th' ant 'eap if you
             wanna.

DOLLY   [*giving him the pills*] Come on, take these.

             He refuses.

             Or would you sooner go an' 'ave a needle in the hospital,
             eh?

             He takes them.

             You wanna cuppa tea? Ay Uncle, wanna *mahngk*?

WORRU   *Kia.*

             He wipes his nose with his hand. DOLLY *gets his
             handkerchief and catches him just before he blows his
             nose bush fashion on the floor.*

DOLLY   Ah, don't do that.

             *She attempts to wipe his nose but he snatches the
             handkerchief and pushes her away. She goes to the sink
             and begins to make a cup of tea.*

WORRU   Ay, where did that fella go?

DOLLY   What fella?

WORRU   You know, Milbart, 'e come 'ere.

DOLLY   When did 'e come here?

WORRU   Dinnertime.

DOLLY   Oh, Uncle Worru, he's been dead *koora, kwotjut noych*, he died Moore River.

WORRU   *Yuart*, 'e come 'ere talkin' to 'im in there.

DOLLY   It's all in your mind, Uncle, an' that's because you been drinkin' again.

She makes the tea, WORRU *shakes his head as if trying to clear his mind.*

I remember that old man. Us kids used to go out robbin' beehives with him.

WORRU   Yeah! Yeah! [*Laughing.*] I remember bee stung you on the *tjenna* once, down Kunjaberrin swamp, an' I 'ad to carry you 'ome on me *moorlin*, nearly six mile. You was real *tjuelara* bony fella, but you was cruel 'eavy for little *yorga*.

DOLLY   Yeah. [*Laughing.*] Ay, Unc? Uncle Worru? You remember Billy Kimberley?

WORRU   Ole Billy Kimberley, *kia*, not young Billy; that old man was *moorditj* with a *kylie*. He could make it go three times 'round that football ground and come back right near his *tjenna*. An' he used to ride that 'orse, 'member Black – Black 'abit. [*Clapping his hands and laughing.*] An' when 'e used to ride that 'orse you couldn't see him at night 'cause 'e was black and the 'orse was black. Proper *moornawooling*, them two. *Kia.* [*Laughing.*] An' when 'e used to ride up the river the kids used to hide in the bushes and call out '*Wahrdung... Wahrdung...* Black Crow... Black Crow...' an' he used to allus carry a long *gidtji*, nor'-west one, an' he would ride over to them boys and yell out, 'Which boy call me black crow, which boy call me black crow?' And them boys would laugh and *doogeearkiny* down the river.

They laugh.

Yeah, but 'e was bad man, Billy Kimberley. Some of them trackers was real *warrah*, you know when them *yorgas* was sent to work for *wetjalas*. [*Miming a pregnant woman.*] And sometimes they would come back *bootjari*, and when them *koolongarahs* was born, them trackers, Billy Kimberley and Bluey too, [*miming choking*] they would *woort beerny* them babies an' bury them in the pine plantation, night time.

DOLLY   Oh, no Uncle Worru, is that true?

WORRU   *Kia kunarn, kunarn!*

DOLLY   What 'appened to them fellas?

WORRU   The *kwotjut nyoch*, finish. Yeah, lotta fellas finish here, Mogumber, Dulung, Binyl, Marrio, Jigalong, Winarn. You remember Winarn, ol' fella with *doot* arm? [*Chuckling.*] Yeah, yeah, he pinched a bottle a whisky from his boss an' he got cruel drunk 'an 'e rolled in the fire and burnt his arm right off – [*pointing*] this one, no, no, that one.

DOLLY   [*laughing*] U-n-c-l-e!

> SHANE, MEENA *and their* Wetjala *friend* DARREN *enter and sprint across the stage outside the house playing keeping-off with a basketball.*

WORRU   Warrah Place, Mogumber, awright daytime, but *gnank weerdiny*, couldn't walk around, stay near the fire. [*Shuddering.*] Too many *tjennaks*, *moorlies*, an', an' *widartjies*. [*Gesturing north.*] They come from that way. They was real bad. Round face, an' they was white, just like *Wetjalas*, an' they 'ad red eyes, an' red 'air, an' them scream, an' shout, sing out in the night time, in the pine plantation, jus' like *koolongahs*.

> SHANE *pushes* DARREN *through the door and throws the ball to him.* DARREN *falls and yells as he catches it.* WORRU *and* DOLLY *get an enormous fright.*

Allewah!

DOLLY   *Choo! Choo!* You frightened the livin' daylights out of me.

DARREN   Sorry.

           SHANE *and* MEENA *enter*.

SHANE   [*laughing*] Sorry, Mum.

DOLLY   What are you chuckin' the ball around the house for?

SHANE   We was just playing keepings off Meena.

DARREN   I'm sorry, Mrs Wallitch.

DOLLY   It's all right.

MEENA   Did you get a fright, Popeye?

WORRU   *Kia*, thought he was bloody *widartji*.

MEENA   Chuck it here.

SHANE   Hey Mum? Anythin' to eat, I'm starvin'.

MEENA   Me too.

DOLLY   Bread and butter and some Vegemite there.

           MEENA *begins to butter slices of bread.*

SHANE   [*pushing in*] Hurry up. Gawd you're slow.

MEENA   Aw, just wait. You're not the only one that's hungry.

WORRU   [*to* DARREN] Ay, boy.

DOLLY   And spread some for Darren too, Shane.

WORRU   Ay, ay, boy.

SHANE   I will, soon as she gives me the knife.

WORRU   Ay, ay, boy.

           He beckons to DARREN *who walks gingerly up to him.*
           You *Wetjala* or *Nyoongah*?

DARREN   What?

SHANE   Hey, Popeye, he's a *Wetjala*.

MEENA   You don't see *Nyoongahs* with red hair, Popeye.

           They laugh. SHANE *and* MEENA *eat ravenously.*

DOLLY   Didn't you kids have lunch?

SHANE   Aw, yeah.

DOLLY   What did you have?

SHANE   We had a pie.

MEENA   Yeah, and he ate three-quarters of it. Eh, Mum, they were all drinking here at lunchtime. [*Pointing to* WORRU.] Him too.

> WORRU *pretends to sleep.* DARREN *moves closer and stares at him.*

DOLLY   Yeah, I know, I know.

SHANE   Where's Dad?

DOLLY   [*laughing wryly*] He went out that door.

> DARREN *continues to stare at* UNCLE WORRU *from close range.* WORRU *suddenly roars and makes an ineffectual grab at him.* DARREN *gets a fright and jumps behind* SHANE *for protection.*

SHANE   Let go, he's all right, he won't hurt you.

MEENA   [*laughing*] Oh, Popeye.

DOLLY   Uncle Worru, don't scare him like that.

WORRU   [*beckoning to* DARREN] Ay boy. Come 'ere, *wetjala*, come 'ere.

SHANE   [*pushing him*] Go on, go on, he won't hurt you, go on, talk to him.

WORRU   Ay. [*Pointing to his beard.*] Do you know what this is, *Nyoongah* way? This is my *gnarnuk*. [*Pointing to his nose.*] This my *moorly*. [*Pointing to his eye.*] And this my meow. [*Indicating his forehead.*] And this my *yimmung*. [*Cackling with delight.*] Plenty *nyoondiak* there, *kia*, plenty *nyoondiak*.

> MEENA *picks up the ball.*

DOLLY   [*beginning to prepare supper*] Oh, I forgot to get tomatoes. Meena, Meena!

MEENA   [*bouncing the ball*] Yes, Mother.

DOLLY   Will you go down an' get me some tomatoes?

MEENA   OK.

DOLLY   [*giving her some money*] Here. Get me a kilo.

SHANE   We'll come with you. Can we get a bottle of cool drink?

DOLLY   I s'pose, an' don't be long.

SHANE   Thanks, Mum. [*To* DARREN.] Come on.

           The children appear at the front bouncing the ball.
           SHANE *intercepts the ball and throws it to* DARREN. *The*
           following conversation is punctuated by a game of
           keeping-off. Inside, DOLLY *makes damper.*

DARREN   Hey, that old man, is he for real?

SHANE   He sure is.

DARREN   How old is he?

SHANE   Must be nearly a hundred.

MEENA   Nah, no he's not, he's about eighty.

DARREN   What language did he talk?

MEENA   Oh that's just *Nyoongah* talk.

DARREN   Can you talk it?

SHANE   Nah, not really.

DARREN   What did he mean by noon... noon...

MEENA   *Nyoondiak*? That means brains.

DARREN   What was for eye?

           MEENA *and* SHANE *look at each other blankly.*

MEENA   I dunno.

           She giggles.

SHANE   Don't ask me, I wouldn't have a clue. I know what *Wetjala*
           is, that's you!

           MEENA *grabs the ball and runs.*

MEENA   Come on you two, Mum said hurry.

           They exit.

WORRU   [*cackling with glee*] That *Wetjala nop* got a cruel fright.

DOLLY   [*kneading the damper*] That wasn't nice, Uncle Worru.

WORRU   Ain't he ever seen a *Nyoongah* before?

DOLLY   *Nyoornditj*, he's a *winyarn*.

           WORRU *laughs dismissively.*

           Wasn't you ever frightened, when you was little?

WORRU   *Kia*. Plenty times and I know you used to be when you was a little fella at Mogumber. You *koolongarah* used to sleep together like puppy dawgs all covered with blankets from head to foots, even 'ot nights.

DOLLY   Yeah, I remember.

WORRU   Good place summertime, *moorditj*, plenty *dytje*, honey, berries and them *kohn*, big like that, taste like 'taters.

DOLLY   And them summer beetles, [*holding her thumb and forefinger about five centimetres apart*] they used to be that long and us girls used to get a piece of cotton from the sleeves of our dresses and tie notes on their legs and throw the beetle up in the air and they would fly away and we wished some boy would find them and read the notes. [*Laughing.*] That's how I met Roy. I don't know whether to be thankful for that beetle or not.

>   *They fall silent.* DOLLY *puts her hand on* WORRU*'s arm.* PETER *enters and saunters across the stage outside the house carrying a leg of kangaroo.*

And you know that was the last time I saw a corroboree at Moore River.

WORRU   [*excitedly*] *Kia, kia*, the *yongarah* dance, the *waitj* dance, the *karda*, the *yahllarah*, the *middar*, the *nyumby*, the *nyumby*... the *nyumby*. *Yuart*, they all finish now, all gone.

DOLLY   Never mind, Uncle, you're still with us, you're *moorditj*, you gonna live to be one hundred.

PETER   [*bursting in*] Hi, look what I got.

DOLLY   Where d'you get that from?

WORRU   *Yonga, woolah!*

PETER   Got it from Aunty Peg.

DOLLY   That'll come in handy.

WORRU   You gotta bacon cook with that?

DOLLY   I'll get some, Unc. [*Feeling the roo.*] My, young one too, nice and tender. Now Peter, I want you to go down and phone up my request.

PETER   Right, who's it to?

DOLLY   To Auntie Rose and the boys at Gnowangerup.

PETER   Reggy and Zac still in gaol, Mum.

DOLLY   I thought they done their time.

PETER   Nah, Zac got moved to Pardellup and Reggy was out on parole but he broke it and now he's back in again.

DOLLY   You write it out, you know how to do it.

PETER   [*writing on his arm*] From Dolly, Roy, Peter...

DOLLY   Better put Eli in.

PETER   ...Eli, Shane and Meena Wallitch.

DOLLY   And Uncle Worru.

PETER   ...and Uncle Worru. [*Reading.*] To Auntie Rose and the boys at Gnowangerup and Reggy at Woorooloo and Zac at Pardellup. Hey, what song?

DOLLY   'Me and Bobby McGee', Charlie Pride. Now go down and ring up straight away, and bring some bacon back and don't mess around now 'cause I need that bacon for supper.

> *She gives him some money. He walks to the door.*

And make sure you read it out nice and clear over the phone.

PETER   Yeah, OK.

> *Peter walks across the stage counting the money and exits.* WORRU *stands up and stretches.*

WORRU   I think I go *bitjarra gnoorndiny* for a little while.

DOLLY   Yes, Unc, you go and have a rest. I'll wake you up supper time.

> WORRU *wanders into his bedroom and lies down.* DOLLY *dusts the damper, places it in the oven and washes her hands.* WORRU *mumbles to himself, gradually becoming louder and more coherent.*

WORRU   Milbart, Milbart, Milbart! *Gidjti wah*, Milbart. Make a spear, I wanna catch a *kulkana*. Make spear, Milbart! *Gidjti wah!*

> *Didjeridoo crashes in, the lights change. The* DANCER *appears at front of stage and in stylised rhythmic steps*

searches for a straight stick, finds it, straightens it, pares and tips it before sprinting up the ramp onto the escarpment and striking the mirrolgah *stance against a dramatic sunset as the music climaxes and cuts.*

SCENE SEVEN

Dusk, still hot. Cicadas drone in the background. WORRU *is asleep in his bed. A pot of kangaroo stew simmers on the stove.* MEENA *sits on the sofa completing an elaborate project.* SHANE *is sprawled on the floor struggling with geography homework.* DOLLY *is sweeping. She pushes* SHANE *aside, sweeps under him and continues on.*

SHANE   Meena! Hey, Meena?

MEENA   What?

SHANE   What's the capital of Wales?

MEENA   [*absorbed in her own homework*] Cardiff.

SHANE   What?

MEENA   Card-iff.

             SHANE *writes carefully.*

DOLLY   Meena, Meena?

MEENA   [*sighing*] Yes, Mum.

DOLLY   Get a bit of newspaper.

MEENA   OK.

             She reluctantly gets some newspaper and uses it as a pan for her mother to sweep the dirt into.

SHANE   What's the capital of London? Meena! What's the capital of London?

MEENA   Aw Mum, he's gotta be joking.

DOLLY   Why?

MEENA   Didn't you hear what he said? How dumb can you get?

SHANE   OK, I just asked a question.

MEENA   Now listen, Shane, London is the capital city of England.

SHANE   Oh.

          Pause.

          Where's Eden-berg?

MEENA   Where?

SHANE   Eden-berg.

MEENA   I dunno, give us a look.

SHANE   See. You don't know everything.

MEENA   Edinburgh, stupid – the capital of Scotland and Ireland. The country is spelt I-R-E-L-A-N-D, not I-S-L-A-N-D.

SHANE   [*resentfully*] I dunno.

          He throws the homework book down, unfolds a comic and begins reading.

DOLLY   Meena, take that rubbish out and put it in the bin. Come on, there's enough flies in here already.

MEENA   Aw, Mum, make Shane do it. I gotta finish a ten-page assignment on Aborigines tomorrow.

          ROY *enters, slightly drunk, and walks across the stage outside the house.*

DOLLY   All right Shane. Come on, Shane!

SHANE   All right.

          He takes it out, still reading his comic.

          Dad's coming!

          ROY *enters the house sheepishly.* DOLLY *ignores him. He walks across to the stove.*

ROY   Eh, I can smell 'roo. Where did you get that from?

DOLLY   Sister Peg give it to me.

ROY   What? No bacon?

DOLLY   No. I sent Peter down for some two hours ago. Did you see him down there anywhere?

ROY   No.

DOLLY   What about goin' down see if you can see where he is.

ROY   Ah, he'll be all right, stop fussin', woman.

DOLLY   All right.

ROY   Anyway, he's most likely with Eli.

DOLLY   Forget about the bloody bacon then.

MEENA   Eh, Pop?

ROY   Yeah.

MEENA   I just worked out something amazing you know how Aborigines have been in Australia for at least forty thousand years, right?

ROY   So they reckon.

MEENA   And if there was three hundred thousand here when Captain Cook came, that means that... that... hm, hang on, hang on...

SHANE   Come on, what's the big news then?

MEENA   Shut up you... listen... forty thousand years plus, three hundred thousand people, that means that over twelve million Aborigines have lived and died in Australia before the white man came.

ROY   Dinkum?

SHANE   Oh boy, they must've shot a lotta 'roos and ate a lotta dampers.

MEENA   They didn't shoot them.

SHANE   I know! Three dampers a day for forty thousand years, how many's that, Pop?

ROY   I dunno, better ask your mother.

DOLLY   Me, I wouldn't have a clue.

MEENA   You don't count it up like that, slowly. Anyway, flour is white man's food. Aborigines used grass seeds. [*Reading from a book.*] Jam seeds, wattle seeds, and –

DOLLY   [*removing the damper from the oven*] OK. Who wants a feed instead of just talkin' about it?

SHANE   [*jumping up*] Me!

          He sprints to the table. DOLLY *intercepts him.*

DOLLY   Go and ask the old bloke if he's getting up for supper.

          SHANE *goes out to* WORRU*'s bed and attempts to wake him.* DOLLY *and* MEENA *serve the stew.* ROY *breaks up the damper.*

ROY   [*sniffing his stew*] Wonder where that boy got to?

SHANE   Popeye?

DOLLY   You said not to worry about him.

SHANE   Popeye?

DOLLY   Remember?

SHANE   Ay, Popeye!

ROY   How much money did you give him?

DOLLY   Two dollars.

SHANE   You getting up for supper, or you wanta eat it in here?

WORRU   What?

ROY   Bet he met up with that bloody Eli and they're down at the Exchange.

SHANE   You getting up for supper, Pop?

WORRU   *Kia.*

DOLLY   Just listen who's talkin'.

          SHANE *helps* WORRU *into the kitchen.*

SHANE   We got 'roo and damper for supper, Pop.

          ROY *starts to eat.*

WORRU   *Woolah, yongah, kwobinyarn, kwobinyarn.*

DOLLY   Roy, you say grace.

SHANE   Do we only say grace when we are eating kangaroo?

ROY   [*putting his spoon back on his plate and swallowing*] We thank you, Lord, for what –

WORRU   You put some bacon in this?

ROY   We thank you

WORRU   Bacon, *wah*?

SHANE   Ssh, ssh, Popeye, close your eyes.

ROY   We thank you, Lord.

WORRU   What for? Can't eat with me eyes closed.

ROY   We thank you, Lord, for what we have got.

WORRU   [*to* SHANE, *pointing upwards*] I forgot about that fella up there.

ROY   Oh, Gawd!

WORRU   *Choo, kynya*, shame, eh?

> *They all laugh, except* ROY *who tries again.*

ROY   [*yelling*] All right, shut up! [*Guiltily.*] We thank you, Lord, for what we got for... your sake an' ours too.

DOLLY   Amen.

WORRU   *Kia.*

> *They eat in silence.* DOLLY *suddenly jumps up and turns the radio on. It is the Earl Reeve 6WF Tuesday Night Country Music Request Programme: Jimmy Little singing 'Baby Blue'.*

> *Winjar mahngk?*

DOLLY   Meena, fill this mug up for him.

> *They eat.* MEENA *pours* WORRU*'s tea.*

MEENA   Popeye, why do *Nyoongahs* call that one *mahngk?*

WORRU   Eh?

MEENA   That one Popeye. Why do *Nyoongahs* call it *mahngk?*

WORRU   That's his name. You see leaf on a tree, that's a *mahngk*, that one *mahngk* too, tea leaf.

> ELI *enters wearing an eye patch and strides across the stage outside the house, carrying a flagon of port.*

MEENA   That's gotta go in my project.

> *She scribbles in her pad. They return to hearty eating.* ELI *enters, sighs and sits at the table.*

ROY   Where's d'you come from?

DOLLY   Did you see Peter?

ELI   The Exchange.

> DOLLY *places a meal in front of him.*

ROY   What'd I tell you?

DOLLY   Did you see Peter?

ELI   Yeah.

ROY   Where's the bacon?

ELI   What fuckin' bacon?

DOLLY   Where is he?

ELI   I think he's up at the police station.

ROY   What?

DOLLY   What for?

ELI   I dunno, he was in a car with a mob of young blokes. Anyway *manatj* pulled 'em up and bunged 'em all in the rat van.

ROY   Where was you?

ELI   They never seen me, I kept outa the road.

ROY   Yeah, trust you.

ELI   What did you expect me to do? You know the bastards don't like me.

ROY   I don't blame 'em.

DOLLY   All right, that's enough, come on.

MEENA   Was probably a stolen car, Mum.

DOLLY   I know. [ROY *prepares to pour himself a drink.*] You put that down, you're comin' with me.

ROY   Aw, you and Meena go, love. What can I do? Y'know I can't talk.

DOLLY   You get on your bloody black feet and walk right out that door.

ROY   All right!

         They leave. MEENA *leaves the table and continues with her homework.* ELI *pours two mugs of port.*

WORRU   Where they goin'?

ELI   Aw, they just gone to see where Peter is. They be back drecktly.

>ROY *reluctantly follows* DOLLY *across the stage.*

ROY   A night in the lock-up would do him good.

ELI   'Ere, get this into you, Unc.

DOLLY   No son of mine is goin' to gaol, not if I can help it.

>DOLLY *and* ROY *exit.*

WORRU   *Kia, kia.*

ELI   [*pointing to his eyepatch*] Yeah, me and old patchy had a good day, Pop.

>*He takes it off and puts it in his pocket.*

WORRU   Patchy?

ELI   Yeah, we were doin' all right outside the shopping centre today, yeah, gettin' fifty cents a bite. One *wetjula* bloke, hippy, he give me two dollars.

WORRU   *Kia*, two dollar.

ELI   Anyways, some of them *Nyoongahs* spotted me. There they was: 'Give me fifty cents, brother', 'Give me a dollar, nephew', 'Give me fifty cents, uncle' and you know none of them black bastards are related to me. That's true. Pop, I never seen blackfellas like 'em, they real bloody dinkum out and out bludgers. Can't stand the bastards.

>WORRU *knocks back his port and pours another.* ELI *turns the radio to full volume.* MEENA *looks up from her homework.*

MEENA   Do you have to have it that loud?

ELI   That's a solid song. Jimmy Little... 'Baby Blue'.

>ELI *sings along drunkenly and pretends to play a guitar.*

MEENA   Wouldn't want to be in your shoes when Mum comes home.

>*She storms out with her project and gets up on* WORRU*'s bed.*

ELI   [*laughing stupidly*] I take 'em off, then.

>*He flings his shoes about the room and settles down with* WORRU *to an evening's drinking as Earl Reeve announces* DOLLY*'s request. 'Me and Bobby McGee'*

fades with the lights. Clap sticks are heard and the
DANCER *appears sitting cross-legged on the escarpment*
against a deep night sky.
    He sings, accompanying himself with the clap sticks.

DANCER *Wahra biny, wahra biny,*
    Koor Ndillah boorndilly doniny.
    Yoongoo bootjahrahk kippulyiny kippulyiny,
    Mahri wahrabiny, wahrabiny, wahrabiny,
    Woolah!

    [Look at the clouds rolling, rolling,
    Thunder crashing, smashing.
    The rain has soaked the earth.
    Clouds rolling, rolling, rolling, Hoorah!]

    The lights snap out on the final beat.

SCENE EIGHT

It is 12.15 am. The radio is crackling. SHANE *is asleep on sofa.* ELI *is stretched out snoring on the floor.* MEENA *is asleep in* UNCLE WORRU*'s room.* UNCLE WORRU *is attempting the overwhelmingly difficult task of pouring himself a mug of port from the flagon. He seems to spend hours trying to direct a few splashes into his mug. He eventually drops the mug on the floor.*

    DOLLY, ROY *and* PETER *enter, walk wearily across the stage and go inside. They stand just inside the door and survey the devastation.*

DOLLY Oh, no...

    WORRU *greets them with a clumsy gesture and an*
    unintelligible grunt. ROY *turns the radio off.* WORRU
    babbles incoherently.

    [*to* PETER, *pointing to* SHANE] Wake him up. Put him to
    bed.

PETER Eh, Shane... Come on, wake up, brother.

SHANE Uh... uh... uh.

PETER   Come to bed, come on.

            He guides SHANE *off.*

SHANE   What happened to you?

PETER   Aw nothin', I'm awright.

            DOLLY *starts to clean up the mess.* WORRU *babbles on.*
            DOLLY *goes out to* WORRU*'s room and attempts to wake*
            MEENA. PETER *returns.*

ROY   [*to* PETER] Gimme a lift with the old bloke.

DOLLY   Meena. Come on, Meena.

ROY   Come on young fella, *tjen kooliny.*

DOLLY   Wake up, Meena.

ROY   *Gnoorndiny* for you.

MEENA   Aw, aw, what's happened?

DOLLY   Nothing, come on.

            MEENA *sleepily follows* DOLLY *into the kitchen.* ROY
            and PETER *eventually drag* WORRU, *who is paralytic*
            and uncooperative, to his feet and attempt to direct him
            towards the door.

ROY   Gawd the old bugger's heavy.

WORRU   [*yelling*] Ay, ay, *winjar koorl,* where we goin'? *Gnuny*
            nooniny barminy.

            He thrashes about and elbows ROY *in the stomach.* ROY
            folds up.

            Ay, leave me alone, *gnuny nooniny bahkininy.*

            WORRU *bites* PETER *viciously on the forearm,* ROY
            grabs WORRU *who is about to topple.*

PETER   Oh, geez, he bit me.

ROY   Come on Peter, give us a hand. Come on, Popeye, what's
            the matter with you.

            They eventually get him, struggling all the way, through
            the door and dump him on his bed. MEENA*'s homework*
            is trampled underfoot. ROY *attempts to gather it up and*
            returns to the kitchen with PETER. DOLLY *throws a*

blanket over ELI.

WORRU Fuckin' bastards.

MEENA [*to* ROY] What happened?

ROY Ask him.

MEENA [*trying to put her homework back in order*] Well?

PETER Got picked up for ridin' in a stolen car.

MEENA What did you get in it for?

PETER Aw, I didn't know it was stolen. Anyway, they said they would drive me home, and I just got in the car when wheek! – the cops pulled us up.

MEENA What time is it?

DOLLY It's about half past twelve.

MEENA Aw, gawd. I'm goin' to bed. Good night, everybody.

She goes.

PETER Me too.

He begins to walk off, stops, takes a packet of bacon of his pocket and drops it on the table.

Mum, Dad, thanks for gettin' me out.

ROY *raises a clenched fist.* PETER *exits.* ROY *looks at* DOLLY, *points to the flagon then to* DOLLY. *She nods.* ROY *pours the last of the port into a mug. The lights fade. He passes it to* DOLLY. *She drinks and passes it to* ROY. *Blackout.*

SCENE NINE

A narrow beam of light reveals WORRU *alone downstage.*

WORRU You have turned our land into a desolate place.
We stumble along with a half white mind.
Where are we?
What are we?
Not a recognised race.

There is a desert ahead and a desert behind.

The soft distant sound of children singing a tribal song is heard. The tribal family of Scene One walk slowly back across the escarpment against a night sky. They are in chains.

The tribes are all gone,
The boundaries are broken;
Once we had bread here,
You gave us stone.

We are tired of the benches,
Our beds in the park;
We welcome the sundown
That heralds the dark.
White lady methylate
Keep us warm and from crying,
Hold back the hate
And hasten the dying.

The tribes are all gone,
The spears are all broken;
Once we had bread here
You gave us stone.

The light on WORRU *fades out. The singing becomes louder as the family disappears and the sky fades to black as the song finishes.*

ACT TWO

MOORGA – WINTER

SCENE ONE

A cold wet winter afternoon. The kitchen/living room is shabby and untidy, dirty dishes piled up on the sink, rubbish, bottles, cigarette packets on floor. Clean clothes are draped over a chair in front of a single bar radiator. WORRU*'s bed has been turned around, his room is squalid.*

An eerie traditional chant as the family of Scenes One and Nine of Act One trudge across the escarpment against a bleak, wintry sky. The women lead carrying an assortment of boxes and bundles. They are inadequately dressed in blankets and shabby period clothes.

As the sound fades and they disappear, a light builds on WORRU *lying on his bed moaning and mumbling a mournful litany, half English, half* Nyoongah. *He coughs painfully, raises himself and staggers feebly into the kitchen.*

WORRU   Ay! Ay! Dolly. *Winjar? Winjar noonak?* Aw, aw, aw, Shane! Shane! Where that *nop*? Shane? Shane?

   He flops into a chair, exhausted.

Dolly, Dolly.

   MEENA *enters and walks briskly across the stage outside the house carrying a school bag.* SHANE *follows, occasionally kicking her bag deliberately to annoy her.* WORRU *lifts himself up and staggers across to the sink and attempts to get a mug of water. He fails, staggers back to his chair, falls into it and collapses limply onto the table.* SHANE *and* MEENA *enter the house noisily.*

SHANE   Hi, everybody!

He stops in his tracks when he sees WORRU.

Meena!

They run across to him and try to wake him.

Popeye, Popeye! It's me, Shane. You all right, Popeye?

WORRU *groans.*

Oh, what did they have to leave him on his own for?

MEENA Push him back, steady, steady.

SHANE Come on, Popeye.

MEENA How are you? You feel all right?

WORRU *groans.*

You sick, Popeye?

WORRU *grunts.*

Shane, go and get a wet towel, quick!

He panics and runs the other way to the sink.

Hurry, Shane!

SHANE All right, don't panic.

They mop WORRU*'s face and sit him up straight. He responds.*

WORRU Where's your mother?

SHANE She's comin' back today.

WORRU Where'd she go?

MEENA She went up to Woorooloo, to see Peter.

WORRU Where *baal kooliny*?

MEENA What, Popeye?

SHANE She's stayin' in Northam at Auntie – what's her name?

MEENA Auntie Elaine.

WORRU Who?

SHANE Auntie Elaine!

MEENA Never mind, he wouldn't know.

WORRU [*angrily*] 'Course I know, she got one of the Stacks, old Harold's boy, Alfie.

MEENA   Popeye, you want a drink of tea?

WORRU   Ay?

MEENA   Want a *mahngk*?

WORRU   No... give me water.

> *She goes to the sink.*

I'm *minditj, koong minditj*.

> *He rubs his side.* MEENA *puts the cup to his lips, he drinks then coughs violently and splutters water everywhere.*

MEENA   I think we'd better put him back in bed, get him by the arm. We gonna take you back to your bed Popeye.

> *He resists, pushing her away.*

You tell him, he'll get up for you.

SHANE   [*putting his arms around* WORRU] Come on, Popeye. We want you to go and lay down. Then we make you nice big cup of tea.

WORRU   [*painfully getting up*] All right.

> SHANE *guides and struggles with him to the door.*

SHANE   I'll take him, you put the pot on.

> *They stumble through the doorway.*

MEENA   Watch out he don't fall.

SHANE   It's all right. [*Putting him to bed.*] Here, wait. I'll fix your pillow for you.

> SHANE *covers him.* WORRU *pushes the blanket off.*

Don't chuck the blanket off, Popeye!

WORRU   It's too 'ot. *Karlawoorliny*.

> SHANE *patiently puts the blankets over him again.*

SHANE   S'not, it's cold.

> SHANE *enters the main room shaking his arms.*

Phew, he's heavy. I'm getting ready for footy practice.

> *He exits.*

MEENA   Plenty of time, we can't go anywhere till they get home.

SHANE   *[off]* Did you wash my footy shorts?

MEENA   Yeah.

SHANE   *[entering]* Where are they?

MEENA   Here!

> *She gets them off the chair in front of the radiator and throws them to him.*

Here!

SHANE   *[feeling them]* They're wet!

> *He holds them in front of the radiator.* MEENA *folds and re-arranges her clothes.*

MEENA   Geez, so are these.

SHANE   What, are you going out tonight?

MEENA   Yeah, later maybe.

SHANE   With your boyfriend?

MEENA   I haven't got a boyfriend.

SHANE   What about Ross Mumblin?

MEENA   What about him?

SHANE   You've been out with him every night since Mum's been away.

MEENA   So what?

SHANE   You wanna watch it.

MEENA   Why?

SHANE   He might be a relation, you know we got hundreds of 'em.

MEENA   Nah, his lot come from Wyndham, somewhere up there.

SHANE   *[laughing]* Yeah, he'd have to with a name like that.

> *The noise of a car is heard in the distance.* SHANE *lacing his football boots.*

Is that his car?

MEENA   Yeah.

SHANE   Has he got a licence?

MEENA   I dunno, s'pose he has.

SHANE   Thought you had basketball practice tonight.

MEENA   Nah, not going.

SHANE   You better stop home tonight. I think Popeye's pretty sick.

MEENA   Yeah, I know.

SHANE   You better wait until they get home.

MEENA   They'll be drunk, anyway.

SHANE   Yeah, Social Service cheques today.

> *A car pulls up outside, doors slam.* SHANE *runs across to the sink and peers out.*

Hey, might be Mum.

> DOLLY *and her nephew,* ROBERT, *enter and walk across the stage.* ROBERT *carries a suitcase, he is in his mid-twenties and smartly dressed.*

MEENA   Nah, too early, bus don't get in till six o'clock.

SHANE   Nah, it's Mum, it is, she must have got a lift with someone.

MEENA   Who?

SHANE   I dunno.

MEENA   Probably Uncle Alf.

SHANE   No... it's a young guy. Hi!

> DOLLY *and* ROBERT *enter the house.*

MEENA   Hi, am I glad you're home.

DOLLY   [*laughing*] Hullo, hullo. Shane, Meena, you know who this is, your cousin Robert, Auntie Elaine's eldest boy. He drove me home.

ROBERT [*shaking hands with* SHANE] Hi. [*Shaking hands* MEENA.] Hi.

DOLLY   You should remember him, he was stayin' with us when we was at Grass Valley.

MEENA   Yeah, ah, I think so.

ROBERT Oh yeah, I remember you all right, you're the one that stuck your big toe in the bobtail's mouth.

MEENA   [*embarrassed*] Oh, yeah.

DOLLY   [*laughing*] You went round and round with that *yuron* stuck to your toe.

ROBERT Think that poor old bobby got more of a fright than you did.

SHANE Hey Mum, did you see Peter?

DOLLY Yeah... he's all right... he's gettin' fat. How's Popeye Worru?

Silence.

Is he all right?

SHANE He's been sick, Mum.

DOLLY Where is he?

SHANE He's out the back in bed.

MEENA He's got a pain in his side. [*Demonstrating.*] Round here. I was just making him a drink of tea.

She makes the tea.

DOLLY Better see how he is.

SHANE Aw, he's probably asleep, Mum, we've just got him to bed.

DOLLY *goes out to* WORRU*'s room.*

ROBERT What, you got footy practice?

SHANE Yeah.

ROBERT Who do ya play for?

SHANE Aw, South Midland, under fourteens, but I barrack for Swan Districts. Narkle brothers, they're solid, eh?

ROBERT Yeah, solid.

DOLLY *returns.*

DOLLY He's sleeping. Has he been taking his medicine and his pills?

MEENA Yeah, Shane gives it to him, he won't take it from anybody else.

SHANE What's the time?

ROBERT Four forty-eight.

SHANE Geez, coach'll murder me.

He picks up his wet shorts.

ROBERT Where you got to go?

SHANE   Bassendean.

ROBERT   I'll run you there.

SHANE   Will you? Oh boy... hang on while I get my gear.

ROBERT   I'll drop into Auntie Peg's and bring him back later.

           SHANE *sprints out.*

SHANE   See you.

ROBERT   See you later, Auntie Bobtail.

DOLLY   See youse later.

           SHANE *and* ROBERT *leave and jog across the front of the stage.* MEENA *re-arranges her clothes in front of the radiator.*

SHANE   Do you play footy?

ROBERT   Yeah.

SHANE   Who for?

ROBERT   Railways.

SHANE   What position?

ROBERT   Rover, usually.

           They exit. DOLLY *sits down.* MEENA *wipes up at the sink.*

DOLLY   What about that cuppa tea?

           MEENA *pours two mugs of tea.*

MEENA   Mum, Robert's solid, eh?

DOLLY   Yeah, he's a nice boy; smart, and he's got a good job.

MEENA   What's he do?

DOLLY   He's a legal aid officer. He's seeing someone in Perth while he's here and he's gonna try and get Pete out on work release.

           MEENA *checks and re-arranges her clothes again.*

           I thought you had basketball practice Thursday nights?

MEENA   I have, but I told them I wouldn't be there tonight.

DOLLY   Why?

MEENA   I don't feel like it.

DOLLY   All right, if you don't feel like it, you can help me clean this place up. Looks like a flamin' rubbish tip.

          She hands the broom to MEENA.

MEENA   Aw Mum, I'm goin' out.

DOLLY   What, with them Yorlah girls again?

MEENA   No I'm not, as a matter of fact, I'm not.

DOLLY   I saw the youngest one down the car park and she was drunk, drunk as a monkey.

MEENA   Well, that's her, not me.

DOLLY   I dunno why you can't get some decent friends instead of those barefooted blackfellas you muck around with all the time.

MEENA   I don't muck around with them all the time. I said I wasn't going out with them, didn't I?

DOLLY   Who are you going out with, then?

MEENA   Ross.

DOLLY   Ross, Ross Mumblin?

MEENA   Yeah.

DOLLY   Where are you goin'?

MEENA   To the drive-in.

DOLLY   What are you goin' to see?

MEENA   [*shrugging her shoulders*] I dunno.

DOLLY   Why don't you get yourself a decent boyfriend like Robert?

MEENA   Aw Mum, he's my cousin.

DOLLY   I know that, but somebody like him. He's gotta good job, nice car.

MEENA   What's wrong with Ross's car? He's got a V8 panel van and he's done it up real nice, got an airconditioner, stereo, bed and... and...

DOLLY   Yeah, I bet he has. You make sure you're home by ten o'clock.

MEENA   Ma-am, the pictures don't finish till after eleven.

DOLLY   You be home by 11.30.

MEENA   Oh gawd, I don't know what you got against Ross, Mum.
         He doesn't even drink.

DOLLY   It's not the drink I'm worried about. Look, I seen girls,
         young girls, younger than you walkin' around with babies
         on their hips and I don't want that happening to you, my
         girl.

MEENA   Aw Mum, what do you think I am, a slow learner or
         something?

DOLLY   I don't, but you've had a pretty fair crack of the whip and
         it's time I started puttin' my foot down.

MEENA   Uh-ah!

DOLLY   You been comin' home late at nights far too often the last
         couple of months.

MEENA   I haven't done anything wrong.

DOLLY   I didn't say you had, but I notice you're always too bloody
         tired for school next day.

MEENA   Aw Mum, why can't I leave school, anyway?

DOLLY   What do you want to leave school for? So you can lay
         around doin' nothing? You're goin' to school for another
         two years, you can get that into your head.

MEENA   I'm not gonna lay about. I'm gonna get a job, Mum.

DOLLY   What sort of a job are you going to get? In the
         supermarket, in a factory? Look, you've got enough brains
         to get a good job, you're smart in school, you get good
         marks, good reports. You could stay on at school and get
         an Aboriginal study grant and really make something of
         yourself.

MEENA   Like what?

DOLLY   Get a decent office job, or become a nurse.

         WORRU *appears in the doorway, jacket off, coughing
         painfully, a pitiful sight in his grubby singlet, baggy
         trousers and bare feet.*

         Hullo, Uncle, how are you?

He sways precariously. She jumps up and runs to his aid.

Oh gawd, Meena, help him.

They gently shepherd him across the room and into a chair.

MEENA   Come on, Pop, steady.

WORRU   [*to* DOLLY] No good, *warrah, nitjal koong minditj.*

DOLLY   How long has he been like this?

MEENA   Oh he's been OK. He just seems to get sick night time.

DOLLY   Go and get a blanket for him. You feel cold Uncle?

No reply.

Noonuk gnitiung?

WORRU   Ugh... yeah.

MEENA *returns with the blanket and carefully drapes it over his shoulders. She walks over and collects her jeans from in front of the radiator and moves the radiator closer to* WORRU.

MEENA   I'm gettin' ready.

She exits to her room.

DOLLY   Like an orange, Uncle? All the way from Sawyers Valley, lovely and sweet.

He feebly puts out his hand, she gives him an orange. He sits there holding it.

I seen old Harold up in Northam.

WORRU   *Winjar?*

DOLLY   In Northam, poor old Harold, [*holding her palm at the level of her stomach*] he got a *gnarnuk* down here.

WORRU   Ah, he's only young fella.

He laughs and coughs.

I kick his arse when he was a little fella.

They both laugh, his laugh becomes a nasty cough. She puts a handkerchief to his mouth, then takes the orange from him firmly.

DOLLY   Gimme that, Unc. I cut it up for you, it'll stop you from coughing. Hey Unc, you get your pension next week and I'm gonna buy you some singlets, new ones to keep you warm. You want white ones or black ones?

WORRU   Black ones, like me.

DOLLY   And we'll get you some new hankies.

WORRU   *Kia*, white ones.

        DOLLY *laughs.*

        Next week I go to Pinjarra.

DOLLY   What for?

WORRU   See *Nyoongah* doctor.

DOLLY   Yeah, good idea, I'll get Robert to drive us down there.

        WORRU *eats a piece of orange.* DOLLY *unsuccessfully searches for food.* MEENA *appears dressed to go out.*

MEENA   Mum, you got any money, couple of dollars?

        DOLLY *searches in her purse and hands* MEENA *one dollar.*

DOLLY   I'll give you a dollar, it's all I got to spare. Gotta buy tucker, can't depend on your father to bring anything home.

MEENA   Bye Pop, bye Mum.

DOLLY   Midnight, remember.

MEENA   OK.

        MEENA *leaves, walks across the stage and exits.* WORRU *attempts another piece of orange but gives up. It falls into his lap.*

DOLLY   Ay Uncle, you feel all right?

WORRU   Yeah, I'm all right, I go *gnoorndiny*.

DOLLY   [*lifting him*] Yeah, come on Uncle, you go and lay down.

        She guides him to his room.

        I'm going down the shop to get some *merrany* and *dytje*. You have a sleep, I'll bring your supper in later.

        She puts him to bed, covers him up and returns to the

kitchen. She turns off the radiator, collects her handbag and leaves. As she walks across the stage counting her money, WORRU *begins mumbling to himself, gradually building to a disturbed cry.*

WORRU   Milbart, *Winjar noonak?* Make a *kaal. Gnuny gnitiung. Witjar gnank weerdiny,* Milbart. *Gnuny* wanta *kaal koong dookan gnoordiny.* Milbart *yuarl nyinaliny gnoordiny.* Milbart *yuarl nyinaliny gnullarah.* Milbart *kaal wah.*

[Milbart, where are you? Make a fire. I'm cold and the sun is going down. I want to lie with my side to fire. Milbart, are you coming to lie down with me? Milbart, come here to me. Milbart, make a fire.]

Didjeridoo crashes in, the lights change. The DANCER *appears at front of stage and in stylised rhythmic steps searches for stone flints, finds them, builds and ignites a fire. Carefully he lifts the fire in cupped hands and carries it to the escarpment where he blows it gently, igniting a careful fire, and sits warming himself against a dark night sky as the music climaxes and cuts.*

SCENE TWO

A short while later WORRU *is home alone, sleeping in his room. Offstage in the distance* ELI *can be heard singing 'Onward Christian Soldiers'. He appears, sways drunkenly across the stage, stops and attempts to count his money. Notes and coins extracted from various pockets fall on the floor. He nearly topples over as he picks them up.*

ELI   Ten dollars and eighty one cents! Not bad, Hawkeye, not bad at all.

He pulls his eye patch down and addresses an imaginary passer-by.

Got bad eyes, boss, this one got catarac', this one goin' fast. Can you spare forty cents, boss? God bless you, sir,

God bless you, missus. [*Gesturing skywards.*] The Big boss! You up there! You listenin'? Hope you been givin' out some of them blessin's I been promisin' them *wetjalas*.

He removes the eyepatch, puts it in his pocket and heads for the house singing 'Onward Christian Soldiers'. He enters the house and looks about.

Hey! Anybody 'ome? Anybody 'ome? I bet them blokes slipped me up on purpose.

He drops into a chair and tears the wrapping from a flagon of VO invalid port and downs a drink.

Well, they don't know I got this. [*Singing.*] Onward Christian Soldiers, marching on –

He stops abruptly.

Ay? 'ow can you be a soldier an' a Christian? Lot a rot; soldiers used to chuck Christians to the lions. I'm a Christian, Freo Prison Christian. Ain't nobody gonna chuck me to the lions. The *Wetjala's* a lion, he eats. Aw, he eats, he eats everything land, trees, rivers, forests, even people, 'specially people. I 'member old grandfather Kooroop used to say: 'Don't trust the *Wetjala*, he's a real *widartji*. He'll kill you for sport and eat your brains and kidney fat.' Poor old grandfather.

ROY enters and walks across the stage carrying a flagon. ELI pours another mug of port and begins singing 'Yes, Jesus loves me'. ROY enters, ELI attempts to hide his flagon under the table.

ROY   Nobody lubs you. Anyway, what did you leave me for?

ROY pours himself a drink.

ELI   I never left you, you left me. [*Holding out his mug.*] Pour me a drink.

ROY   Why?

ELI   'Cause I want a drink.

ROY   What's that under the table?

ELI   That's a flagon of VO. I'm savin' that for us later.

ROY   Ah, this is good ol' Valencia.

ROY *pushes the flagon across to* ELI *and takes out a packet of tailor-made cigarettes and fumbles about unsuccessfully for matches.*

Give us the matches.

ELI   Ain't got any.

ROY *stumbles across to the sink, looks for matches, and spots* DOLLY*'s suitcase.*

ROY   Jesus!

ELI   What?

ROY *gestures at the suitcase.*

Oh, Lawd.

ROY   She musta went down the street.

ELI   [*staring at his watch*] Northam bus only just gettin' in.

ROY   She musta gotta lift.

ELI   Who with?

ROY   Musta been one of Elaine's boys.

ELI   Not that smart arse, Robert?

WORRU *wakes, sits up suddenly and cries out.*

WORRU   Ay! Ay! Milbart! *Winjar noonak!*

ROY   Go and see what he wants.

ELI   He's got a good nose, that old fella, he smelt this.

ELI *goes to* WORRU*'s room.* WORRU *drops on to his bed and mumbles to himself.*

WORRU   Milbart, *yuarl nyinaliny gnullarah.*

ELI   Ay old fella, you all right.

WORRU *grunts and coughs.*

Ay, Unc, you want a *kaep*?

WORRU   No, *yuart.*

ELI   What, you *minditj*, Uncle?

WORRU   Yeah, no good, no good, I go Pinjarra tomorrow, me and Dolly.

ELI   Yeah, what you goin' there for, Uncle, gunna see some of your old girlfriends?

WORRU [*dropping off to sleep*] Go Pinjarra, see *Nyoongah* doctor.

ELI Sure, Uncle, you have a *gnoorndiny* now, Aunty Dolly be 'ome drecktly.

He returns to the kitchen.

'E's still talkin' about the *Nyoongah* doctor, lotta bullshit.

ROY I dunno, might do him some good.

ELI Balls.

ROY Don't worry about that, I seen some good things done by some of them fellas.

ELI Yeah, what?

ROY Once them *nyoongahs* was fightin' on the six acre reserve at the Williams' and old Morden got his 'ead split open with a *doak* an' Yinell, he was *boolya* man, he got some of that green slimy stuff from the river and packed it all around 'is 'ead and he was good as ever. [*Laughing, miming a boxer.*] He come back lookin' for more of this.

DOLLY *enters and walks across the stage carrying a small bag of groceries.* ELI *fills the mugs.*

ELI I still reckon it's a lotta bullshit.

ROY *Nyoongahs* never went to *Wetjala* doctors in them days. They was frightened of 'em.

ELI Yeah, that's why so many of 'em fuckin' died.

DOLLY *enters, stops in the doorway and surveys the scene.* ROY *does his best to appear sober.*

ROY Aw, 'ullo love, 'ow you goin'? Didn't know you was 'ome.

ELI Yeah, spotted your bag.

ROY [*to* ELI] Shut up! [*To* DOLLY.] 'E's drunk.

DOLLY [*putting the groceries away*] Same old homecomin'.

ROY 'Ow d'ya get 'ere, on the bus?

DOLLY No, Robert brought me 'ome.

ELI I thought so.

ROY Has 'e gone back?

DOLLY   No.

ELI   [*under his breath*] Worse luck.

DOLLY   He took Shane to footy practice.

   DOLLY *goes through her suitcase.*

ROY   'Ow's Peter?

DOLLY   Aw, 'es all right, he's puttin' on weight. 'Ere, he sent this for you.

   She presents him with a fancy leather stubby holder.

   Made it himself, it's a stubby holder.

ELI   Shoulda been a flagon holder.

ROY   Well, 'e'd 'ave to make you one too.

ELI   Gawd I'm hungry. What's for supper, Auntie?

DOLLY   You're gettin' polony sandwiches.

   DOLLY *strides across to* ROY, *puts her hand out and flips her fingers.*

   Come on, come on, you know what: *boondah.*

   ELI *laughs,* DOLLY *turns on him.*

   You too, Eli. [*To* ROY.] Come on, come on, stand up.

   ROY *stands. She goes through his pockets.*

ELI   You got more pockets than a pool table.

   DOLLY *counts the money.*

DOLLY   You shut up, Eli, your turn next. Ah, sixty bucks, wonders will never cease.

ROY   [*laughing*] Ha, ha, you missed one, you missed one.

DOLLY   Come on, come on, how much you got in it, come on, how much?

   ROY *produces a dollar.*

   You can keep that.

   She turns on ELI *and puts out her hand.*

ELI   You won't have to search me, Auntie, I'm as honest as the day is long.

DOLLY   Come on, Eli, forty, come on.

She dips her hand into his pocket.

ELI   Ay, Auntie, no, *choo*, this one's Patchy, this one SS pocket.

A car is heard pulling up, doors shut. ROBERT *and* SHANE *enter and walk across the stage.* SHANE *has a football and* ROBERT *a carton of beer.*

DOLLY   I don't care which pockets you get it out of as long as I get it.

ELI *reluctantly produces a handful of notes which he drops.* DOLLY *scoops them up quickly.*

Ah, that's rent and tucker for the next couple weeks anyway.

DOLLY *stuffs the money down her bra.* ROBERT *and* SHANE *enter the house.*

ROY   Ay, 'ow you goin' neph'?

ROBERT   Good, Unc, how are you?

ROY   I'm OK.

SHANE   What's for supper?

DOLLY   I'm makin' sandwiches drecktly. Gawd, look at you. You better go and have a shower, you're filthy.

ROBERT   [*to* ELI] How are you, Eli?

ELI   Aw, not bad.

SHANE   Aw Mum, I couldn't do a thing right at practice, I got dumped every time.

ROBERT   Don't worry, mate, I told you everybody has their off days.

ELI   Ah, you should 'ave me for a coach.

ROBERT *and* SHANE *are playing handball.*

ROY   [*pensively*] Dinkum?

ELI   Look, I tell you, I played full forward for Federals in Wagin. One match I kicked ten goals, right through the big sticks.

He demonstrates.

ROY   Full forward. [*Laughing.*] Full and forward, belly up to the

	bar and then you got kicked right outa the pub.

ELI   OK. Give us it here, I'll show you how to handle a football. Come on, come on, punch it 'ere, come on, punch it 'ere.

SHANE   Right. Lead, cousin Eli, lead!

>   SHANE *punches the ball to him hard. It hits him in the stomach, he falls awkwardly, winded. Everyone laughs.*

ELI   [*puffing*] Ay, ay, fair go. I wasn't ready, come on, come on.

>   *He sets it up to punch it back but* ROBERT *flicks it out of his hand.* ELI *raises his hand to strike him.*

DOLLY   All right, come on you boys, steady down.

SHANE   Give us the ball.

DOLLY   I'll have the ball before youse break something.

>   ROBERT *passes the ball to* DOLLY.

SHANE   Put it under my bed, Mum, I'm gonna have a shower.

>   *He exits.*

ROBERT   [*to* ELI] You couldn't get a kick in a stampede.

ELI   Yeah? I was the only one what gave the scoreboard fellas cramp.

ROBERT   Must have been from laughing at not changing the scores.

>   WORRU *suddenly lets out a mournful wail.*

WORRU   Ay, Dulong, Benyi, Winarn, coooo – ooh!

DOLLY   Oh Lawd.

>   *They all stand transfixed looking towards his room.*

ROBERT   Let's have a look, Auntie.

>   ROBERT *runs into* WORRU*'s room.* DOLLY *follows.* WORRU *appears to be asleep.*

          You OK, Uncle?

DOLLY   Uncle Worru, you all right?

ROBERT   He's asleep.

>   DOLLY *puts a blanket over him, they return.*

ROY   What's up with him?

DOLLY   I dunno, must 'ave been talkin' in his sleep.

ROBERT   He's OK.

DOLLY   He reckons he wants to go to Pinjarra next week.

ROBERT   What for?

DOLLY   He wants to see the *boolya* man.

ROBERT   Don't worry Auntie, I'll drive you down there.

ELI   Waste of fuckin' petrol money, if you ask me.

ROBERT   I'll be paying for the petrol, not you.

ELI   Why don't you take him up here where you been takin' him for the last four or five years?

DOLLY   They'll only keep him there. You know how he hates hospitals.

ELI   I still reckon he's better off in hospital than someone mumblin' a lot of blackfella bullshit over him.

ROBERT   Can't you see the old bloke believes in it? It's not going to do him any harm. It's faith healing, purely a case of mind over matter, auto-suggestion. Call it what you like.

ELI   You call it what you like, I call it bullshit.

DOLLY   [*to* ELI] Pipe down, you.

ROY   [*laughing*] Let 'em go, let 'em go.

ROBERT   Now you take the Bible, the story of Noah's Ark. It would have been physically impossible for Noah to transport every species of animal on earth for forty days and forty nights.

ROY   Oh, that's my nephew. You're solid, neph'. Keep goin', keep goin'.

ROBERT   [*pointing at* ELI] And to prove it even more –

ELI   [*knocking his hand*] Don't you fuckin' point at me.

           He twists ROBERT*'s finger.*

ROBERT   [*stepping back*] To prove it even more, Noah would have had to have a staff of thousands to feed all those animals and look after them.

ELI   Yeah, well you listen, you think you know everything. What about them big boats come into Fremantle? They take thousands of sheeps and take 'em to other countries. If those fellas can do it, Noah coulda done it.

ROBERT   The point is because thousands of people for thousands of years have believed in the story of Noah's Ark, they believe through faith. You see what I mean, Auntie?

DOLLY   [*uncertainly*] Yeah.

ROY   Well, I don't.

ELI   He's talkin' out of his *kwon*. If it's in the Bible it's bloody true.

ROBERT   Listen coz, belief in the Bible is based on faith, not fact.

He points, ELI *grabs his finger and twists it hard.*

Hey! Cut it out.

ELI   I told you not to point, didn't I? [*Twisting it viciously.*] Didn't I?

ROY   Come on, cut it out, cut it out.

DOLLY   That'll do! That'll do! Stop it, you two.

WORRU *sits up and lets out another harrowing wail.*

WORRU   Milbart, coooo – oooh!

ELI *lets go of* ROBERT *'s finger.*

ROY   Lawd, not again.

DOLLY *runs to his room.*

WORRU   Benyi, plenty *yongarah* there, Milbart? Fresh water? [*Laughing heartily.*] *Woolah*! I come *boordah-woon, kia, kia.*

DOLLY   Ay, Uncle?

WORRU   What?

DOLLY   You all right?

WORRU   Yeah, I'm good.

DOLLY   You lay down, cover yourself up.

WORRU   Nah, I'm goin' drecktly.

DOLLY   Where you goin'?

WORRU   That-a-way, *bo-oh-oh.*

ROBERT   Is he OK?

DOLLY   Yeah, he reckons he's takin' off drecktly.

ROY   You wanta watch him, love, he might do that.

DOLLY   Nah, he'll go back to sleep now.

ELI   Tie him up, Auntie, one leg to the bed.

ROBERT   That's the sort of thing you would say.

ELI   I'm only jokin'. You wanta stop gettin' heavy, mate.

          Robert replies with the 'up yours' gesture

ROY   He'd get loose, he's a cruel strong old man.

DOLLY   Old Uncle Harold was tellin' me a story about oldy, when he was a young bloke workin' on Minilya. The overseer and the boss tied him up and they beat him and belted him with a bleedin' stock whip. They left him there tied up in the sun. Anyway he got loose and night time they was *tjurip* sleepin', he snuck up on 'em and he belted them two *Wetjalas* somethin' cruel.

ROBERT   What happened, did they catch up with him?

DOLLY   No way. Old Harold reckon he done that.

          DOLLY gives the Nyoongah gesture for running off. SHANE appears from the shower with a towel over his shoulders. He makes for the radiator.

          You go and get a shirt on.

SHANE   I'm OK.

DOLLY   Go on, you gotta cold already.

SHANE.   If I can find a clean one.

WORRU   [*calling*] Hey, hey! Shane? Shane boy, come 'ere.

DOLLY   [*to* SHANE] Go and see what he wants. [*To* WORRU.] He's comin', Uncle.

          ELI produces a pack of cards. SHANE goes to WORRU's room.

ELI   Who wants a game?

ROY   OK. How much a hand?

SHANE   What did you want, Popeye?

ELI   [*to* ROBERT] I don't suppose you play cards?

WORRU   Where you been?

ROBERT   I can reef your money off you any day, mate.

          DOLLY *throws a blanket over the table. They sit down and commence the game.*

SHANE   I just had a shower.

ROY   Right, twenty cents jackpot.

SHANE   Eh, Popeye, you look funny sittin' there. Here, I'll comb your hair.

WORRU   You wanna watch out, don't go thatta way.

SHANE   [*laughing*] Yeah, why?

WORRU   You go thissa way, I seen them featherfoot tracks there. Aha, they think they clever fellas, not as clever as me.

SHANE   Yeah, that's right, Popeye, that's right. You lay down.

WORRU   You watch out now.

          SHANE *returns.*

SHANE   Aw Mum, he's talkin' about featherfoots.

DOLLY   Aw, he's been dreamin'.

WORRU   Ay! Ay! Shane, Shane! Come 'ere, come 'ere. Where you is?

SHANE   [*exhaustedly*] Oh no, not again.

DOLLY   Go on, talk to him, I'll bring both youse supper in as soon as I've reefed a dollar off your father.

          She laughs.

SHANE   All right, I'm comin, Popeye.

          SHANE *walks in and sits down beside the old man.*

DOLLY   And Patchy's money off cousin Eli.

          The card game continues in earnest. WORRU *claps his hands.*

WORRU   *Gnuny* gonna sing 'bout them *tjenna guppi.*

SHANE   Yeah, Popeye.

          As he sings, clapsticks followed by didjeridoo take up

the rhythm. The light fades on the kitchen, then on
WORRU *'s room.*

WORRU   *Allewah! Tjenna guppi nyinanliny,*
A nyinanliny, a nyinanliny, nyinanliny,
Mundika nyinanliny,
Mundika nyinanliny,
Ngunyinniny kaka woorniny,
A koka woorniny
Tjenna guppi nyinanliny,
Tjenna guppi,
Tjenna guppi,
Tjenna guppi,
Woolah!

[Watch out, featherfoot there
There, there, there
There in the bushes
There in the bushes
I'm laughing
Laughing
Featherfoot there
Featherfoot
Featherfoot
Featherfoot
Hooray!]

Shafts of cold light fade in revealing the DANCER *as
featherfoot at the front of stage. He is heavily decorated
with leaves and carries two short sticks. He dances
slowly across the stage and up on to the escarpment
and off as the music and lights fade.*

SCENE THREE

A few hours later SHANE *is asleep on the foot of* WORRU*'s bed. The card game continues, empty cans litter the table.*

ELI   I'll bet a dollar.

ROBERT   OK. I'm looking.

DOLLY   I'll have a look.

ROY   [*throwing in his cards*] That's busted me. I'm gonna settle down to some steady drinkin'.

          He picks up a flagon and sways across to the couch. ELI *triumphantly shows his cards.*

ELI   Three fives!

DOLLY   That beats me.

          ELI *reaches for the money,* ROBERT *grabs him firmly by the hand.*

ROBERT   Hold it, hold it coz, three sixes!

DOLLY   Gee, that was a good pot.

ELI   Bastard! Give us the cards.

ROY   Started on Patchy's pocket yet nephew?

          ELI *shuffles the pack.*

ELI   Bloody cards, oughta be chucked in the bloody fire.

ROBERT   You can please yourself, they're your cards. Anyway I'm thirty dollars in front.

ELI   Bully for you. Anyway, it's early yet.

ROBERT   Right, your deal.

          ELI *shuffles furiously and drops several cards. As he picks them up he slips a few cards, unseen, under his leg.*

DOLLY   Come on, you two. Stop snapping at each other. You're like two cats.

ROY   More like two *dwerts*. Eli's a kangaroo dog and Robert's a greyhound.

ELI   Right, who's got openers?

ROBERT   Not me.

DOLLY   No, not me.

ELI   Right, I'll open it for two dollars.

DOLLY   I'm out.

ROBERT   [*to* ELI] You got a pat hand?

ELI   I'm not gonna tell you.

ROBERT   You have to.

ELI   I don't.

ROBERT   He has too, doesn't he, Uncle Roy?

ROY   Don't put me into it, I'm not playing.

ROBERT   That's the rules.

ELI   Look, we're playin' jackpot *Nyoongah* way, not *Wetjala* way.

ROBERT   All right, give me four cards.

ELI   Sure, my little greyhound of a cousin.

ROBERT   All right, all right, what do you bet?

ELI   You want to bet, eh? All right, five dollars!

         They each throw in five dollars. ELI *goes to put his cards down.*

ROBERT   Wait a bit, wait a bit. Back another five dollars.

ELI   Aha, cheeky bugger, eh? Your five.

         ELI *stands up and goes through his pockets.*

DOLLY   Eh, you boys are getting a bit heavy.

ROY   Eh Mum, don't forget to take the light money out of this pot.

         ELI *throws a handful of notes and coins into the pot.*

ELI   And back seven forty! And you can't kick it again 'cause that's all I bloody well got. Aha, beat that, three tens and a pair of nines.

ELI throws his cards down triumphantly. ROBERT *stands and shows his cards one after the other.*

ROBERT One, two, three, four sevens. I don't care whether you're playing *Nyoongah* way or *Wetjala* way, four cards beats a full hand anytime.

ELI Fuck the cards, lend me five bucks.

ROBERT What for?

ELI Lend me five bucks.

ROBERT Here you are. I don't mind collecting it out of your next SS.

ELI Right, come on, come on!

ROBERT *deals.*

DOLLY Well leave me out, I never lost anything. I finished up square.

ROY I only lost a dollar.

DOLLY Yeah, and what I gave ya, don't forget that.

While ROBERT *is dealing* ELI *drops his cards and as he picks them up attempts to substitute some for the ones he is sitting on.* ROBERT *sees him. He stands up and reaches across the table grabbing* ELI *by the shirt.*

ROBERT Eli, you fucking, cheating, black bastard.

DOLLY Oh, Eli.

ELI What's bugging you?

ELI *grabs for the pot but* ROBERT *beats him to it.* ELI *grabs* ROBERT *by the wrist and jerks him violently over the table. Chairs, cards and beer cans go flying.* ROBERT *grabs* ELI *by the hair,* ELI *tries to kick him.*

You got my money there; come on hand it over.

DOLLY *tries to break up the fight,* ROY *tries to rescue the booze and during the chaos* WORRU *falls off his bed.*

SHANE Mum, Mum!

ROBERT I haven't, you stupid idiot.

DOLLY Stop it, stop it you two!

SHANE   [*entering in a panic*] Mum, Dad!

ROBERT   You fucking cheat.

DOLLY   Will you stop it?

SHANE   Popeye's sick!

ROBERT   I lent you five dollars, you ungrateful bastard.

SHANE   Help Mum, Popeye's sick!

　　　　　 DOLLY *runs into* WORRU*'s room. The fight continues.*

ELI   Let go of my hair. Fight like a man, not a bloody woman.

ROBERT   You fight like a bloody horse.

　　　　　 ELI *manages to kick* ROBERT *hard in the leg.* ROBERT
　　　　　 pulls away, SHANE *runs between them crying*
　　　　　 hysterically.

SHANE   Stop fightin'! Popeye's fallen off the bed.

　　　　　 The scene freezes.

　　　　　 The light changes, didgeridoo crashes in a wild
　　　　　 threatening drone. The DANCER, *again as featherfoot,*
　　　　　 appears and moves slowly across in front of them
　　　　　 removing the decorating leaves and leaving them
　　　　　 strewn on the front of the stage. As he exits, the sound
　　　　　 and light fades.

SCENE FOUR

A distant ambulance siren, the hollow footsteps and clatter of a
hospital corridor. A pool of light reveals WORRU, *wrapped in a*
blanket, sitting in a wheelchair. DOLLY *stands beside him.* WORRU
looks about vaguely.

WORRU   Where's everybody?

DOLLY   They're all home, Uncle.

WORRU   *Yuart*, somebody was 'ere.

DOLLY   That was Robert, Uncle.

WORRU   Where's he gone?

DOLLY   He's talking to Sister, filling in some forms for you.

WORRU   [*trying to get up*] I'm not staying here!

DOLLY   [*restraining him gently*] You just stay here for a little while. Next week I take you to Pinjarra.

WORRU   No, I'm goin' that way.

DOLLY   You'll be all right Uncle. Doctor's coming to see you drecktly.

WORRU   Hm! Who's that fella?

DOLLY   What fella, Uncle?

WORRU   [*impatiently*] That *Nyoongah* fella! Bring us here.

DOLLY   Oh Uncle, that's Robert, he's one a' your grannies. He's one of Elaine's boys. They used to stay with us at Grass Valley. You 'member?

WORRU   I know, I know, Grass Valley, all got sent Mogumber.

DOLLY   No, that was before, Uncle, that was *koora*.

WORRU   Yeah, big mob, all go to Mogumber, big mob, 'ad to walk. Toodjay, Yarawindi, New Norcia. Summertime too. Can't go back to Northam, no *Nyoongahs*. *Kia.* I runned away with Melba. [*Laughing.*] Jumped the train at Gillingarra. Went back to Northam, [*miming handcuffs*] *manadtj* got me at the Northam Show. Put me in gaol, Fremantle, for long time. When I went back to settlement Roy was born, [*gesturing*] this big, *kia*, [*laughing*] little fella.

          He laughs and begins to cough painfully. DOLLY *comforts him.*

DOLLY   You talkin' too much, Uncle, you sit quiet now.

          He holds DOLLY *tight by the arm.*

          You sit quiet now Uncle, I'm stayin' right here.

          A nurse enters, looks at DOLLY *and slowly wheels* WORRU *off.* DOLLY *follows.* WORRU *mumbles to himself as the lights fade.*

WORRU   Milbart, Dulung, Benyi, Winarn, Milbart, Milbart.

SCENE FIVE

A few hours later SHANE *is asleep on the couch.* ROY *is sitting staring blankly into space.* ELI *is on his hands and knees clearing up.*

ELI   What a bloody mess.

ROY   You made it, man, you made it.

ELI   I didn't do it all on me bloody own.

> SHANE *stirs and turns over on the couch. A car is heard pulling up outside. One door slams.* SHANE *jumps up half asleep and runs across to the sink and peers out.*

That must be them.

SHANE No it isn't.

ROY   Who is it?

SHANE Oh, its only Meena.

> MEENA *walks across the front of the stage. Her hair and clothes are dishevelled. She puts her shoes on and attempts to tidy herself up.*

She'll cop it when Mum gets home.

ROY   She deserves all she bloody well gets.

> MEENA *creeps silently into the house and stops bewildered.*

MEENA Where's Mum?

ROY   Where have you been?

MEENA Is she in bed?

SHANE No.

ROY   Do you know what time it is?

MEENA [*ignoring him*] Where is she, then?

SHANE Her and Robert took Popeye to the hospital.

MEENA What for?

ELI   Aw, he got crook.

MEENA   Is he all right?

SHANE   Popeye got a fright and fell out of bed.

ROY   Anyway, where have you been? It must be two o'clock in the bloody morning.

MEENA   To the drive-in.

ROY   Till this hour of the morning?

MEENA   We run out of petrol.

ROY   How did you get home, then?

MEENA   Ross's car.

ROY   Thought you said you run out of petrol.

MEENA   We did, but we got some off Jimmy Yoolah.

ROY   You'll need a better excuse than that when your Mother gets home. Have you got enough energy to make me a cup of tea?

MEENA   Aw Pop, I'm tired. I gotta get up and go to school in the morning.

ELI   [*getting up and putting the pot on*] Useless, bloody useless.

ROY   A good clip in the ears would do you the world of good, young lady.

MEENA   You know what's wrong with you, Pop, you got a hang-over.

         She nestles on to the couch next to SHANE.

SHANE   Don't take all the blankets.

MEENA   Gimme some.

SHANE   Aargh, keep the stinkin' blanket.

         He grabs the cushions, makes a bed on the floor and goes to get a blanket from WORRU*'s bed.*

ROY   Why don't you go and get in your own bed?

MEENA   I'm sittin' up till Mum and Popeye get home.

         SHANE *runs from* WORRU*'s room dragging the blanket behind him. He stops, alarmed, and looks behind. They all look at him in silence.*

ELI   What's wrong?

SHANE   Ooh!

             SHANE *stands there and looks at them.*

MEENA   What's up?

SHANE   Something in there.

MEENA   Where?

SHANE   In Popeye's room.

ELI   Ah, you seein' things.

             SHANE *wraps himself in the blanket and curls up on his makeshift bed.*

ROY   Shane, why don't you go to bed?

SHANE   I'm not goin' till I find out how Popeye is.

             ROY *walks slowly out to* WORRU*'s room.*

ELI   Aw, stop worryin', boy, you couldn't kill that old fella with the back of a sleeper axe.

             ROY *stands still in* WORRU*'s room, then walks back with slow measured steps, all eyes are on him.*

             What's the matter?

             ROY *looks at him, doesn't reply but sits and stares blankly ahead.*

MEENA   What time is it?

ELI   About half past two. You want a cuppa tea?

MEENA   No, I wanta sleep. Wake me up when they get home.

             ELI *makes a cup of tea.* SHANE *covers his head with the blanket, the lights fade slowly.*

             A narrow shaft of light reveals the DANCER *sitting cross-legged on the escarpment against a night sky. He sings sorrowfully.*

DANCER   *Nitja Wetjula, warrah, warrah!*
             Gnullarah dumbart noychwa.
             Noychwa, noychwa, noychwa.
             Wetjala kie-e-ny gnullarah dumbart.
             Kie-e-ny, kie-e-ny, kie-e-ny,
             Kie-e-ny.

[The White man is evil, evil!
My people are dead.
Dead, dead, dead.
The white man kill my people.
Kill, kill, kill,
Kill.]

SCENE SIX

A few hours later the first light of dawn silhouettes the house. SHANE
and MEENA *are asleep.* ROY *is dozing in a chair and* ELI *stares
blankly out the window.*

Eventually a car is heard pulling up outside.Two doors close. ROY
wakes. A distant didjeridoo drone begins as DOLLY, *followed by*
ROBERT, *walks slowly across the stage.* DOLLY *is carrying* WORRU*'s
clothes. The didjeridoo builds as they enter the house. They stand in
silence.* ROY *and* ELI *stare at* DOLLY *hopelessly.* DOLLY *puts the
clothes on the table, walks across the couch and wakes* MEENA. ROY
goes to MEENA. SHANE *stirs, wakes and looks about.*

SHANE   Where's Popeye?

          DOLLY *kneels beside him, whispers in his ear and holds
          him in her arms. He cries out, the didjeridoo builds to a
          climax and cuts. Blackout.*

SCENE SEVEN

A single shaft of light reveals DOLLY *alone centre stage. She speaks
slowly with restrained emotion.*

DOLLY   Stark and white the hospital ward
          In the morning sunlight gleaming,
          But you are back in the *moodgah* now

Back on the path of your Dreaming.

I looked at him, then back through the years,
Then knew what I had to remember:
A young man, straight as wattle spears
And a kangaroo hunt in September.

We caught the scent of the 'roos on the rise
Where the gums grew on the Moore.
They leapt away in loud surprise
But Worru was fast and as sure.

He threw me the fire-stick, oh what a thrill!
With a leap he sprang to a run.
He met the doe on the top of the hill
And he looked like a king in the sun.

The wattle spear flashed in the evening light,
The kangaroo fell at his feet.
How I danced and I yelled with all my might
As I thought of the warm red meat.

We camped that night on a bed of reeds
With a million stars a-gleaming.
He told me the tales of *Nyoongah* deeds
When the world first woke from dreaming.

He sang me a song, I clapped my hands,
He fashioned a needle of bone.
He drew designs in the river sands,
He sharpened his spear on a stone.

I will let you dream – dream on old friend
Of a child and a man in September,
Of hills and stars and the river's bend;
Alas, that is all to remember.

   Blackout.

THE END

FURTHER READING

BERNDT R.M. Aborigines of southwestern Australia: the past and the present'. *Journal of the Royal Society Western Australia*, Vol. 56, Parts I and 2, 1973.

BERNDT, R.M. and C.H. BERNDT (eds) *Aborigines of the West: their past and their present*. University of Western Australia Press, Perth, 1980. See chapters 1, 5 to 8, 24.

BISKUP, P. *Not slaves not citizens.The Aboriginal problem in Western Australia, 1898-1954*. University of Queensland Press, St. Lucia, 1973.

DOUGLAS, W.H. *The Aboriginal Languages of the South-West of Australia*. Australian Institute of Aboriginal Studies, Canberra, 1976.

HASLUCK, P. *Black Australians. A survey of native policy in Western Australia, 1829-1897*. Melbourne University Press, Melbourne, 1942.

MCNAIR, W. and H. RUMLEY. *Pioneer Aboriginal Mission. The work of Wesleyan missionary John Smithies in the Swan River Colony, 1840-1855*. University of Western Australia Press, Perth, 1981.

NEVILLE, A.O. 'The "Native Question".' *Science in Western Australia*. Australian Association for the Advancement of Science, 18th Meeting. Government Printer, Perth,1926.

NEVILLE, A.O. 'Relations between settlers and Aborigines in Western Australia.' *The Western Australian Historical Society*, Vol. II, Part XIX, 1936.

NEVILLE, A.O. *Australia's Coloured Minority*. Currawong Publishing Co., Sydney, 1947.

NEVILLE, A.O. 'Contributory causes of Aboriginal depopulation in Western Australia'. *Mankind*, Vol. 4, No.1.

NEVILLE,A.O. *'The half-caste in Australia'* . Mankind, Vol. 4, No. 7., 1951.

GLOSSARY OF ABORIGINAL TERMS

The Aboriginal language used in these plays is usually called *Nyoongah* but occasionally referred to as *Bibbulumun*. *Nyoongah* literally means 'man', but has become a general term denoting Aboriginality in the South-West of Western Australia. *Bibbulmun* is one of the fourteen South-West languages that have combined over the last 152 years to create the modern *Nyoongah* spoken in the play.

ALLEWAH, watch out!
BAAL, them
BAHKININY, bite
BANTJI, banksia
BARMINY, strike
BITJARRA, sleep
BOH-OH, a long way
BOOLYA, magic
BOOLYADUK, one skilled in magic
BOONDAH, money; literally stone
BOONDAH WAH, do you have money?
BOORDAH-WOON, soon, directly
BOOTJARI, pregnant
BRIDAIRA, boss, master
BUKILY, hit
BUNJIN, play around (with women)
CHOO, shame
CHOO KIENYA, real shame
DALYANINY, run away
DOAK, throwing stick
DOOGEEARKINY, flee
DOOKAN, lying on one's side
DOUBLEGEE, a clover burr prevalent in Western Australia
DUBBAKINY, slowly
DUMBART, people of the same tribe

DWERT, Dingo,dog

DYTJE, meat

GIDTJI WAH, do you have a spear?

GNANK, sun

GNARNUK, beard

GNITIUNG, old term for a white man, lit. cold

GNOOP, blood, also wine

GNOORNDINY, sleep

GNOWANGERUP, a South-West country town

GNUMMARI, a mild narcotic root; tobacco

GNUNY, me, I

GOONAMIA, toilet; literally excrement shelter

GUPPI, feathers

JAM, tree of WA, acacia acuminata

JINNA, feet

JUNGARA, returned dead. The Tjuart believed that when they died their *kanya* (freshly departed soul) rested in the *moordgah* tree (*nuylsia floribunda* or Christmas tree) until it departed for *Watjerup* (Rottnest Island) when the tree's vivid orange blossoms die. There it shed its dark skin and appeared white. When Captain Stirling and his party landed, the Aborigines assumed them to be the *jungara* ('the returned'). They assumed the visit of the *jungara* was temporary; some even recognised departed relatives.

KAAL, fire

KAAL WAH, do you have fire?

KAEP, water

KAEP WAH, do you have water, liquor?

KARDA, racehorse goanna

KARLAWOORLINY, hot

KARTA KOOMBA, Mount Eliza, literally 'head that is huge', the highest point in an area surrounded by marshes, plains and the Swan River, with a running freshwater spring at its foot, *Karta Koomba* was probably an important site to the Tjuart clan that occupied the region.

KEERT KOOLINY, going quickly

KIA, KIA, yes yes

KOBBLE, stomach

KOBBLE WEERT, hungry

KOHN, wild potato
KOOLINY, go
KOOLONG, KOOLONGARAH, child, children
KOOMP, urine
KOONG, side, rib-cage
KOORAWOORLINY, an expression of disbelief
KUDDEN, red gum tree
KULKANA, mullet
KULUMAN, (coolamon), basin-shaped wooden dish
KUNARN, the truth
KUNYA, a freshly departed spirit
KWOBINYARN, excellent
KWON, arse
KWOTJUT, in the past
KWOTJUT NOYCH, dead a long time
KYLIE, boomerang
KYNYA, shame
MAHNGK, leaves, vegetation, tea
MAHRI, clouds
MANATJ, police, literally 'black cockatoo'. The dark peak-cap
uniforms of the early police caused them to be compared to this bird.
MARTA, legs
MEOWL, eye
MEOWL BIRT, blind person
MERRANY, damper, flour, bread
MIDDAR, traditional dance
MINDITJ, sick
MIRROLGAH, balance, the act of throwing a spear
MOODGAH, nuystia floribunda, West Australian Christmas tree
MOORDITJ, good
MOORE RIVER, the Mogumber Native Settlement, a State Government
Reserve established in 1918 and closed in 1951.
MOORLIE, unkind spirit
MOORLIN, back
MOORLY, nose
MOORNAWOOLING, black
NIETJUK, who
NITJAL, here

NOONINY, NOONUK, you
NOP, boy
NUMBER NINES, (coll) big feet police
NYINALINY, there
NYINNING, here
NYNGARN, echidna
NYOONDIAK, brains
NYOONGAH, Aboriginal
NYOORNDITJ, a pitiful person
NYUMBY, traditional dance
TJARRALY, jarrah
TJEN KOOLINY, walk
TJENNA, feet
TJENNA GUPPI, featherfoot, executioner
TJUELARA, skinny
TJURIP, pleased
UNNA, isn't it?
WARRAH, bad
WARRAH WANGEING, bad mouthing
WART ARNY YIT, move along
WATJERUP, Rottnest Island
WAYARNING, frightened
WEERDINY, downwards
WETJALA, white person, a corruption of the English 'white fellow'
WIDARTJI, an evil spirit
WINJAR KOORL, where are we going?
WINJAR NOONAK, where are you?
WINYARN, weak willed person
WOOLAH, a shout of praise
WOONANA, behind bars
WOORT BEERNY, to strangle
YAHLLARAH, a traditional dance
YIMMUNG, forehead
YONGA, YONGARAH, kangaroo
YORGA, woman
YUARL, you
YUART, no
YURON, bobtail goanna